Contents

Working Scientifically

Section 1 — Energy and Matter

Section 2 — Forces and Motion

Section 3 — Waves

Section 4 — Electricity and Magnetism

Section 5 — The Earth and Beyond

The Scientific Process

Scientists work scientifically — it's their job. It means they can plan awesome investigations, get useful results and draw scientific conclusions from them. You need to be able to do all that too. Fear not though, this section will tell you everything you need to know. You'll also be tested on Working Scientifically topics throughout this book — look out for questions with a WS stamp: WS

A Hypothesis is an Explanation of Something

1) Scientists observe (look at) things they don't understand.
2) They then come up with an explanation for what they've seen.
3) This explanation is called a hypothesis.

Example:

A scientist is looking at why people have spots.

He notices that everyone with spots picks their nose.

The scientist thinks that the spots might be caused by people picking their nose.

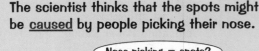

Nose picking = spots?

So the hypothesis is: "Spots are caused by picking your nose."

4) Next, scientists try to work out whether the hypothesis is RIGHT or NOT.
5) They do this by making a prediction and testing it.

You need to be able to make predictions too.

Example: A prediction is something like: "People who pick their nose will have spots."

6) If tests show that the prediction is right, then there's evidence (signs) that the hypothesis is right too.
7) If tests show that the prediction is wrong, then the hypothesis is probably wrong as well.

Other Scientists Test the Hypothesis

1) It's not enough for one scientist to do tests to see if the hypothesis is right or not.
2) That's why scientists publish their results — so other scientists can find out about the hypothesis and do the tests for themselves. Results are published in peer-reviewed journals.
3) Sometimes other scientists will find more evidence that the hypothesis is right.
4) When this happens, the hypothesis is accepted and goes into books for people to learn. An accepted hypothesis is often called a theory.

A journal is a collection of scientific papers. 'Peer-reviewed' means other scientists have checked the results and scientific explanations before the journal is published.

I agree...
New science stuff to learn

5) Sometimes the scientists will find evidence that shows the hypothesis is wrong.
6) When this happens, scientists have to either change the hypothesis or come up with a whole new one.
7) Sometimes new evidence will be found that means an accepted theory needs to change. This is how theories develop.

It's another great book from CGP...

This book contains essential study notes and practice questions for every topic in KS3 Physics (ages 11-14) — perfect for making sure you've really understood the subject.

It's ideal if you're working at a higher level, which would have been called Levels 5-7 in the old Curriculum.

CGP — still the best! ☺

Our sole aim here at CGP is to produce the highest quality books — carefully written, immaculately presented and dangerously close to being funny.

Then we work our socks off to get them out to you — at the cheapest possible prices.

Published by CGP

From original material by Paddy Gannon.

Editors:
Mary Falkner, Gordon Henderson, David Maliphant, Matteo Orsini-Jones

Contributors:
Stuart Barker, Barry Pywell, James Wallis

ISBN: 978 1 78294 112 5

Clipart from Corel®
Printed by Elanders Ltd, Newcastle upon Tyne.

Based on the classic CGP style created by Richard Parsons.

With thanks to Ian Francis, Rachel Kordan, Glenn Rogers and Sarah Williams for the proofreading.

Investigations

Scientists do investigations to find things out. You need to be able to do investigations too...

Investigations Give Us Evidence

1) Scientists carry out investigations to test their predictions and collect evidence to test their ideas.
2) You need to be able to plan and carry out investigations to test your predictions.
3) You can do investigations in a lab (laboratory) or somewhere else. For example...
   - A lab is the best place to study topics like light and electricity.
   - But if you want to investigate changes in atmospheric pressure, you'll need to go outside. This is called fieldwork... although it doesn't always have to be in a field.

Investigations Have to be Fair Tests

1) Before you start an investigation, you need to plan what you're going to do.
2) You need to make sure the investigation you plan will really test whether your prediction is right or not.
3) To do this, you must make sure it will be a FAIR TEST. This means you must...

ONLY CHANGE ONE THING. EVERYTHING ELSE must be kept the SAME.

4) The thing that you CHANGE is called the INDEPENDENT variable.
5) The things that you keep the SAME are called CONTROL variables.
6) The effect that you MEASURE is called the DEPENDENT variable.

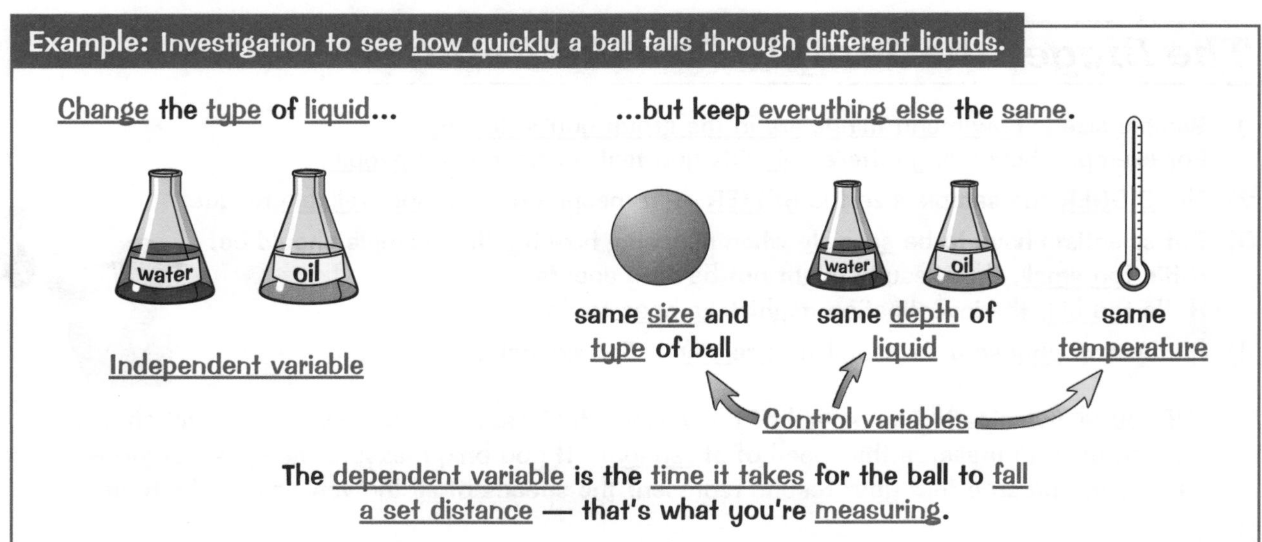
Example: Investigation to see how quickly a ball falls through different liquids.
Change the type of liquid...
...but keep everything else the same.
water
oil
Independent variable
same size and type of ball
water
oil
same depth of liquid
same temperature
Control variables
The dependent variable is the time it takes for the ball to fall a set distance — that's what you're measuring.

The Equipment Has to be Right for the Job

1) You need to choose the right equipment for your investigation.
2) For example, choose measuring equipment that will let you measure stuff accurately.

If you need to measure out 11 cm³, this measuring cylinder would be great. It's the right size and you can see where 11 cm³ is.

This measuring cylinder isn't as good. It's too big and you can't really see where 11 cm³ is.

Investigations Can be Hazardous

1) A hazard is something that could cause harm.
2) Hazards include things like heavy masses, electricity, chemicals and fire.
3) Scientists need to manage the risk of hazards by doing things to reduce them. For example, if you're using a Bunsen burner:

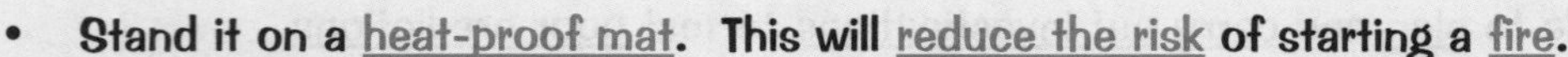

- Stand it on a heat-proof mat. This will reduce the risk of starting a fire.
- Always turn it off or to the yellow safety flame when you're not using it. The blue flame is hard to see, so this will reduce the risk of you injuring yourself.

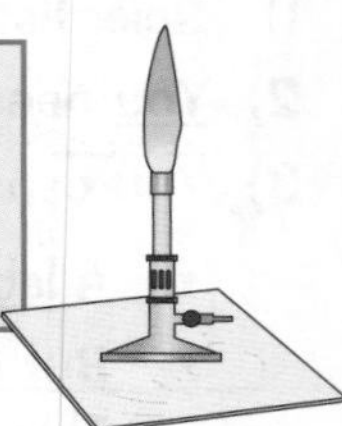

Investigations Need to be Repeated

1) The more times you repeat your investigation the better — but three times is usually enough. Then you can work out the mean (average) — see next page.
2) If you get the same or very similar results each time that you repeat your investigation, that's good news. It means your results are repeatable.

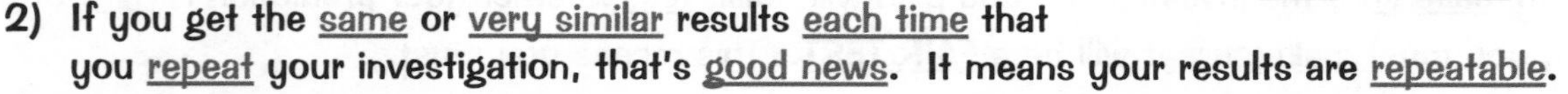

3) It also means that they're more likely to be reproducible by other scientists. If other scientists can reproduce your results, it's more likely that your hypothesis is right (see page 2).
4) Results that are both repeatable and reproducible are said to be reliable.
5) Collecting lots of results and calculating a mean can improve accuracy. Accurate results are really close to the true answer.

The Bigger the Sample Size the Better

1) Sample size is how many things are in the group you're testing. For example, how many different liquids you test, or how many people.
2) The BIGGER the sample size the BETTER — it means you get more reliable results.
3) But scientists have to be sensible when choosing how big their sample should be. If it's too small, their results might not be very accurate. If it's too big, the investigation might take ages to do.
4) It's best to choose your samples at random. For example:

If you're investigating the speed of the vehicles that pass your school, you should choose which ones to measure the speed of at random. If you only measure the speed of lorries, you can't be sure that your results represent the speeds of all the vehicles on the road.

Errors Can Pop Up if You're Not Careful

1) The results of your experiment will always vary a bit because of random errors — tiny differences caused by things like making a mistake when you're measuring.
2) If the same error is made every time, it's called a systematic error. For example...

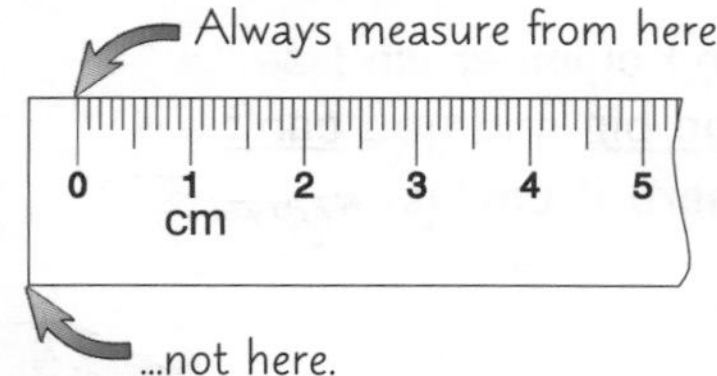

If you measure from the very end of your ruler instead of from the 0 cm mark every time, all your measurements would be a bit small.

Organising and Presenting Data

Once you've collected your results (data) you need to organise and present them nice and clearly.

Data Needs to be Organised

1) Results need to be organised so that they can be processed later on.
2) Tables are really useful for organising data.
3) You should always make sure that each column has a heading and that you've included the units.

Liquid	Time taken for ball to fall 30 cm (s)		
	Repeat 1	Repeat 2	Repeat 3
A	28	37	32
B	47	51	60
C	68	72	70

You Might Have to Process Your Data

1) When you've done repeats of an experiment you should always calculate the mean (average).
2) To calculate the mean add together all the data values. Then divide by the total number of data values.

Liquid	Time taken for ball to fall 30 cm (s)				
	Repeat 1	Repeat 2	Repeat 3	Mean	Range
A	28	37	32	(28 + 37 + 32) ÷ 3 = 32.3	37 – 28 = 9
B	47	51	60	(47 + 51 + 60) ÷ 3 = 52.7	60 – 47 = 13
C	68	72	70	(68 + 72 + 70) ÷ 3 = 70.0	72 – 68 = 4

3) You might also need to calculate the range (how spread out the data is).
4) To do this find the largest result and subtract the smallest result from it.
5) You want your results to be as precise (close to the mean) as possible — so the smaller the range, the better your results.

You Can Present Your Data in a Graph or Bar Chart

1) Presenting your data in a graph or bar chart makes it easier to spot patterns in the results (see next page).
2) Whatever type of graph or chart you draw, you must choose sensible scales for the axes and remember to label them. Make sure you include the units too.

Bar Charts

1) If you're measuring something that comes in categories you should use a bar chart to show the data.
2) Categories are things like type of material or different energy stores. You can't get results in between categories.

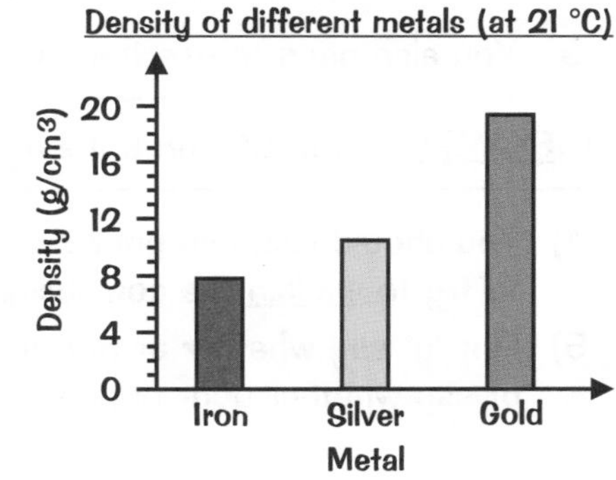

Line Graphs

1) If you're measuring something that can have any value in a range, you should use a line graph to show the data.
2) For example, mass and spring extension could both be shown on a line graph.
3) The dependent variable (the thing you measure) goes on the y-axis.
4) The independent variable (the thing you change) goes on the x-axis.

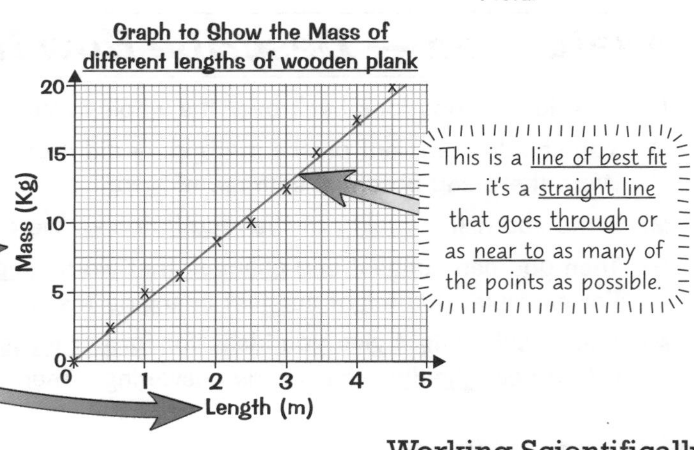

Concluding and Evaluating

Drawing a conclusion is all about finding patterns in your data.

Line Graphs Can Show Patterns in Data

1) When you're carrying out an investigation it's not enough to just present your data — you've also got to find any patterns in the data.
2) Line graphs are great for showing patterns in data.

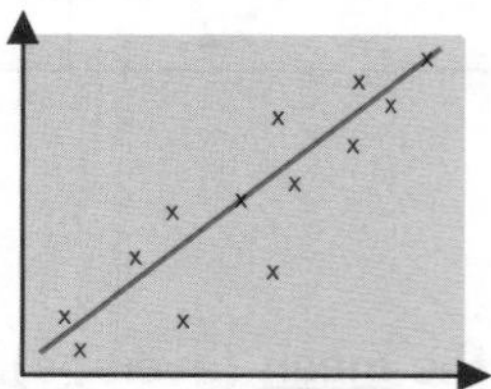

You can see here that as one variable increases the other increases too.

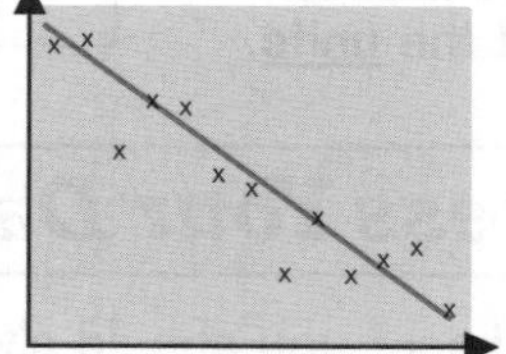

Here, as one variable increases the other decreases.

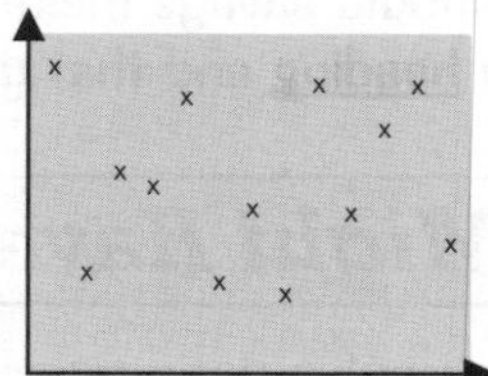

There's absolutely no pattern to be seen here...

A Conclusion is a Summary of What You've Learnt

1) Once you've organised and presented your data, you need to analyse it and come to a conclusion.
2) You just have to look at your data and say what pattern you see.

EXAMPLE: how does the number of turns on an electromagnet affect how many paperclips it can pick up?

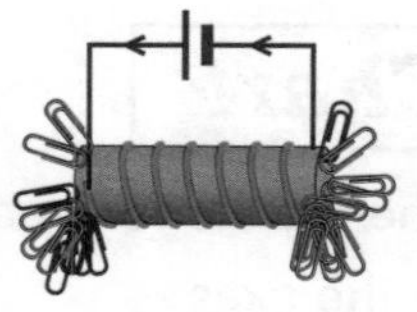

Number of turns of wire	Number of paperclips picked up on average
10	7
15	11
20	14

CONCLUSION: The more turns of wire that there are on an electromagnet, the more paperclips it will be able to pick up.

3) You also need to use the data that's been collected to justify the conclusion (back it up).

EXAMPLE: With 20 turns the magnet picked up twice as many paperclips as with 10 turns (on average).

4) You should also use your own scientific knowledge (the stuff you've learnt in class) to try to explain the conclusion.
5) Finally, say whether or not your results back up your original hypothesis — or say whether your original prediction was right or wrong.

Evaluation — Describe How It Could be Improved

In an evaluation you look back over the whole investigation.

1) You should comment on the method — did it produce reliable results? If not, why not? Were there any potential sources of error?
2) Write about the quality of the results too — were they repeatable and accurate?
3) Then you can suggest any changes that would improve the quality of the results. For example, you might suggest changing the way you controlled a variable.
4) Your results might give you ideas for further investigations too. For example, you might come up with a new question that needs answering. Then the whole scientific process starts again...

Energy and Energy Transfer

Learning Objectives

It's the start of the book, so you'll no doubt be full of enthusiasm and energy. By the time you reach the end of this topic, you should have the energy to...

- understand that energy can be held in different types of energy stores
- describe the transfers of energy an object goes through when it moves, changes shape, changes its chemical composition, changes its position in a field or changes temperature
- describe the energy transfers that take place when an electric circuit is completed
- give examples of situations where an object is transferring energy between different stores.

Energy Can Be Stored

Energy can be held in different stores, such as:

Kinetic (Movement) Energy Store

Anything that moves has energy in its kinetic energy store.

Electrostatic Energy Store

Two electric charges that attract or repel each other have energy in their electrostatic energy stores.

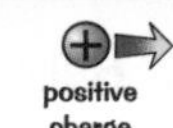

See page 92 for more.

Elastic Energy Store

Anything stretched has energy in its elastic energy store — things like rubber bands, springs, knickers, etc.

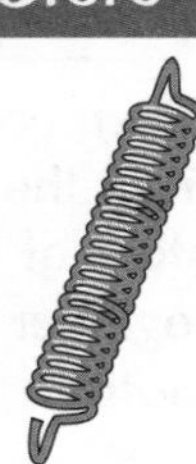

Magnetic Energy Store

Two magnets that attract or repel each other have energy in their magnetic energy stores.

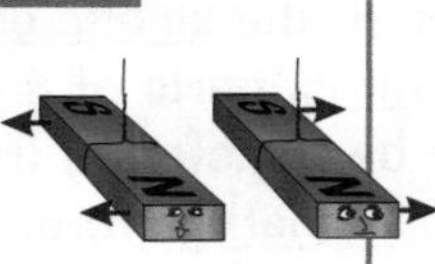

There's more on magnets on page 94.

Chemical Energy Store

Anything with energy which can be released by a chemical reaction — things like food, fuels and batteries.

Thermal Energy Store

Everything has some energy in its thermal energy store — the hotter it is, the higher its temperature and the more energy it has in its thermal energy store.

Gravitational Potential Energy Store

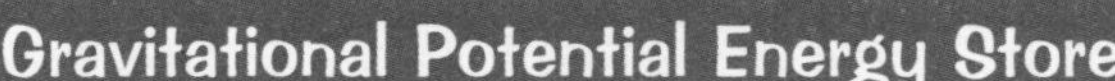

Anything in a gravitational field (i.e. anything that can fall) has energy in its gravitational potential energy store — the higher it goes, the more it has.

In physics, a field is a region in which a particular force can act on objects. So if something's in a gravitational field, it means it's in a region where gravity can act on it.

Energy Can Be Transferred Between Stores

1) Whenever (pretty much) anything happens to an object, energy is transferred from one store to another — the store of energy you transfer to increases, and the store of energy you transfer from decreases.
2) There are four main ways you can transfer energy between stores:

Mechanically

When a force makes something move (see page 10). E.g. if an object is pushed, pulled, stretched or squashed.

By heating

When energy is transferred from hotter objects to colder objects (see page 13).

Electrically

When electric charges move around an electric circuit due to a potential difference (see page 83).

By light and sound

When light or sound waves (see Section 3) carry energy from one place to another.

3) Phew. Here are some examples of energy being transferred between stores:

When you drop an object, it moves through a gravitational field. This causes energy to be transferred from its gravitational energy store to its kinetic energy store.

When you burn fuel, energy is transferred from the fuel's chemical energy store to the thermal energy store of the surroundings.

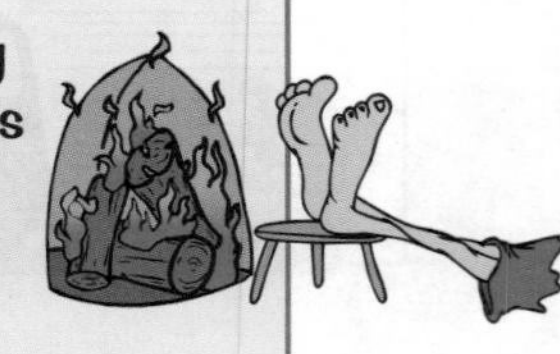

When you switch on this electrical circuit, energy is transferred from the battery's chemical energy store to the kinetic energy store of the motor. Then as the motor turns, parts of it rub together — this causes some energy to be transferred from the motor's kinetic energy store to its thermal energy store.

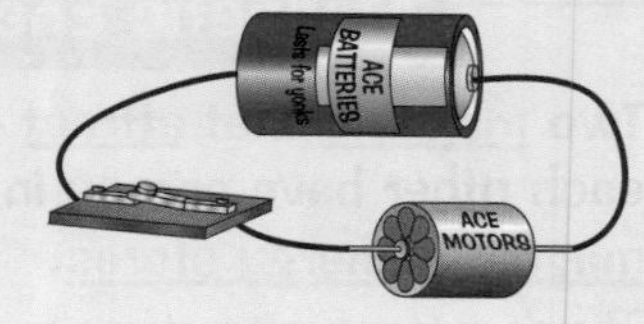

A stretched object, like a spring, has energy in its elastic energy store. When it's released, the energy in the elastic energy store decreases quickly as it is transferred to the kinetic energy store of the object (and anything you're firing).

Food contains energy in its chemical energy stores. When you eat food, it is metabolised (changed during chemical processes inside your body), which releases (transfers) the energy in the food. You can then use the energy for useful things like walking, keeping warm and studying science.

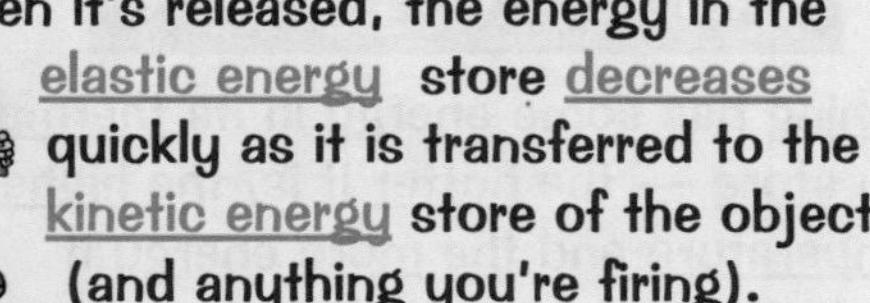

Excessively Entertaining Energy Questions

Quick Fire Questions

Q1 When will an object will have more energy in its thermal store — when it is hot or when it is cold?

Q2 Describe the energy transfer that takes place when a stretched rubber band is released and fired across a room.

Q3 Describe the energy transfers that take place when a bobsled hurtles down a track.

Practice Questions

Q1 Draw lines to join each store of energy on the left to the object containing the **most energy in that store** on the right.

electrostatic	**an athlete running a race**
gravitational potential	**a magnet attracting a pin**
kinetic	**two electric charges repelling each other**
magnetic	**a stationary roller coaster just before a big drop**

Q2 A battery-powered toy crane is holding a wooden block up above the floor. The crane releases the block and it starts to fall.

(a) Tick the correct box to show the energy transfer taking place as the block falls.

☐ From the **gravitational potential** energy store of the **crane** to the **magnetic** energy store of the **block**.

☐ From the **gravitational potential** energy store of the **block** to the **kinetic energy** store of the **block**.

☐ From the **gravitational potential** energy store of the **crane** to the **kinetic** energy store of the **crane**.

☐ From the **kinetic** energy store of the **crane** to the **kinetic** energy store of the **block**.

(b) The crane is then used to lift the block up again from the floor. What **useful** energy transfers take place as the block is lifted? Tick the correct box.

☐ From the **gravitational potential** energy store of the **block** to the **kinetic** energy store of the **block**.

☐ From the **chemical** energy store of the **battery** to the chemical energy store of the **crane**.

☐ From the **gravitational potential** energy store of the **crane** to the **gravitational potential** energy store of the **block**.

☐ From the **chemical** energy store of the **battery** to the **gravitational potential** store of the block.

Q3 Write down the stores that energy is transferred between in the pictures below. (Note that **one** store of energy can be transferred to **more than one** store.)

(a) ....

....

(b) ....

....

(c) ....

....

Topic Review Did you sail through the questions without any trouble? Are you sure you understand all of the learning objectives?   

More on Energy Transfer

Learning Objectives

In the last topic you only scratched the surface of all things energy transfer. By the time you've got through this one, you'll hopefully have no problem...

- knowing that energy is transferred when a force moves an object
- being able to calculate the energy transferred when a force moves an object by a given distance
- understanding that you can use the same amount of energy to apply a big force over a short distance or a small force over a long distance.

Energy is Measured in Joules

1) The standard unit for measuring energy is joules, J.
2) One joule is roughly the energy needed to lift an apple by 1 metre.
3) When a lot of energy is transferred, you can use kJ (a thousand joules).

Energy is Transferred When a Force Moves an Object

When a force moves an object through a distance, energy is transferred.

Energy transferred is the same as work done — see page 54.

1) If you want to move something, you need to supply some sort of force to it.
2) The thing putting in the force needs a supply of energy (e.g. from the chemical energy stores in fuel or food etc.).
3) The force then transfers energy by moving the object — the energy transferred by the force could be transferred to the object's kinetic energy store (if the object's getting faster), to its gravitational potential energy store (if the object's getting higher) or to the thermal energy store of the object and the surroundings (if the object's being pulled over rough ground).

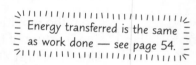

Energy Transferred, Force and Distance are Linked by an Equation

To find how much energy is transferred (in joules) by a force when it moves an object, you just multiply the force in newtons (N) by the distance moved in metres (m).

$$\text{Energy Transferred (in joules, J)} = \text{Force (in newtons, N)} \times \text{Distance (in metres, m)}$$

EXAMPLE: Some yobs drag an old tractor tyre 5 m over rough ground. They pull with a total force of 340 N. Find the amount of energy that they transfer.

ANSWER: Energy transferred = force × distance = $340 \times 5 = 1700$ J

For a Fixed Amount of Energy, More Force Means Less Distance

1) If you give a machine a certain amount of energy to transfer, the amount of force it can apply and the distance over which it can apply it are linked — if one goes up, the other must come down.
2) So the machine can apply a large force over a small distance, or a small force over a large distance.

EXAMPLE: A forklift truck is used to lift crates of CGP revision guides onto a shelf.

Small crates weigh 1000 N and get put on the top shelf, 4 m off the ground.

Large crates weigh 4000 N and get put on the bottom shelf, 1 m off the ground.

Show that it takes the same amount of energy to put away a small crate or a large crate.

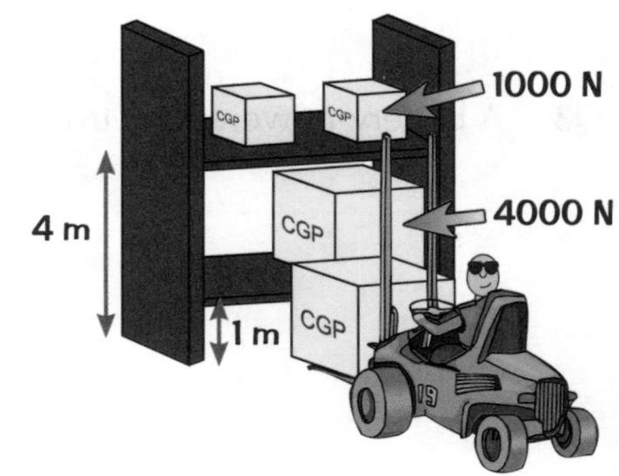

ANSWER: Energy transferred for small crate = force × distance
= 1000 × 4
= 4000 J

Energy transferred for large crate = force × distance
= 4000 × 1
= 4000 J

Extraordinarily Excellent Energy Questions

Quick Fire Questions

Q1 What's the standard unit for measuring energy?

Q2 When a force moves an object upwards through a distance, what type of store is energy transferred to?

Q3 Write down the formula that links energy transferred, force and distance.

Practice Questions

Q1 A model train uses a force of 10 N to pull a carriage at constant speed.

(a) The train pulls the carriage for a distance of 2 m. How much energy does the train transfer? Tick the correct answer.

☐ 5 J ☐ 10 J ☐ 12 J ☐ 20 J

(b) An extra carriage is added to the train. The total force needed to pull the carriages is now 20 N. How much energy does the train transfer over 2 m now? Tick the correct answer.

☐ 10 J ☐ 22 J ☐ 40 J ☐ 42 J

Q2 An arcade machine uses a spring to push a metal ball.

(a) How is energy stored in a spring when it is compressed?

....

(b) When the spring is released, it pushes on the ball with a constant force of 15 N for a distance of 0.2 m. How much energy does the spring transfer?

Energy transferred = ... J

Q3 A battery-powered toy truck is being driven up a slope with a steady driving force of 80 N.

(a) What type of store of energy is the truck transferring energy from as it drives up the slope?

....

(b) Name **two** stores of energy that this energy is transferred to.

....

(c) Calculate the energy transferred by the truck if it drives 15 m up the slope.

Energy transferred = ... J

Challenge Yourself

Q4 Toy car A drives with a steady force of 35 N and covers 2000 m with a fully-charged battery. Toy car B drives with a steady force of 80 N. How far would it be able to drive using the same fully-charged battery as car A?

Distance = ... m

Topic Review

How did you find the questions?
Are you happy with all the learning objectives?

Energy Transfer by Heating

Learning Objectives

It's time to take a closer look at some energy transfer between thermal energy stores. Once you've warmed to these pages, you should know that...

- energy is transferred from hotter objects to cooler objects by heating
- when hot objects transfer energy to cooler objects, the difference in temperature between the two objects drops
- when two objects reach the same temperature, they're said to have reached thermal equilibrium
- when objects are touching they can transfer energy to each other by conduction
- all objects radiate invisible thermal radiation, with hotter objects radiating more than cooler ones.
- insulators can be used to slow down the rate of energy transfer between two objects.

Energy is Transferred From Hotter Objects to Cooler Ones

1) When there's a temperature difference between two objects, energy will be transferred from the thermal energy store of the hotter one to the cooler one by heating. This tends to reduce the temperature difference — the hotter object will cool down and the cooler object will heat up.
2) This carries on until the objects reach thermal equilibrium — the point at which they're both the same temperature.

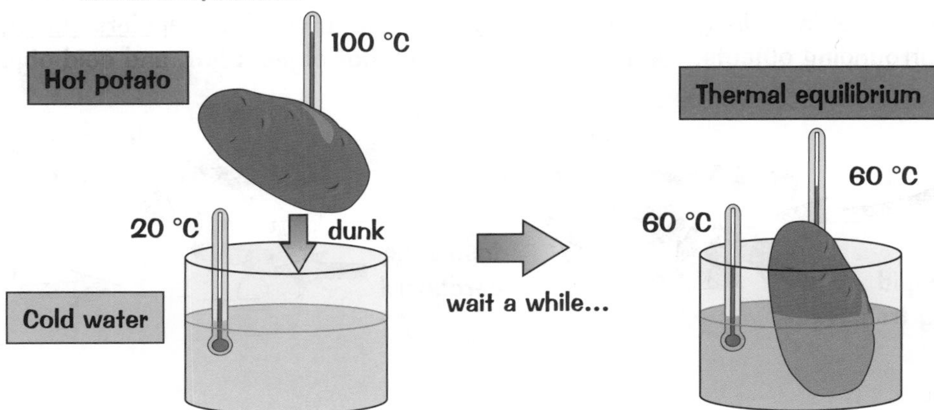

You need to know about two ways in which energy can be transferred between objects by heating:

1) Conduction

1) When an object is heated, the particles in the object vibrate more — energy is transferred to their kinetic energy stores.
2) Conduction occurs when vibrating particles transfer energy to the kinetic energy stores of their neighbouring particles.
3) It only happens when particles can bump into each other, so the objects must be touching.
4) Particles in the hotter object vibrate faster than particles in the cooler object. When the particles in the hot object bump into the particles in the cold object, energy is transferred.
5) The hot object loses energy and cools down, while the cold object gains energy and heats up.

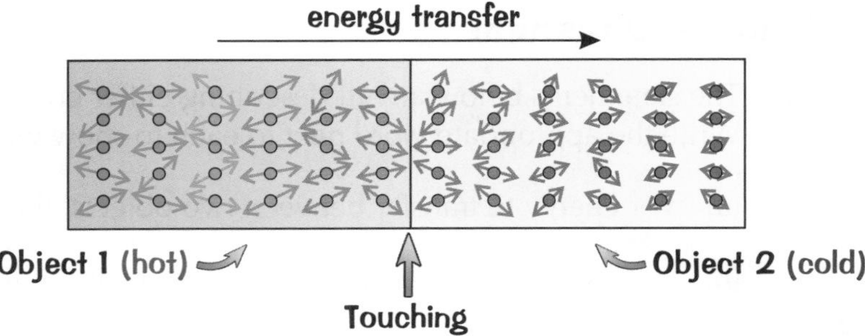

2) Radiation

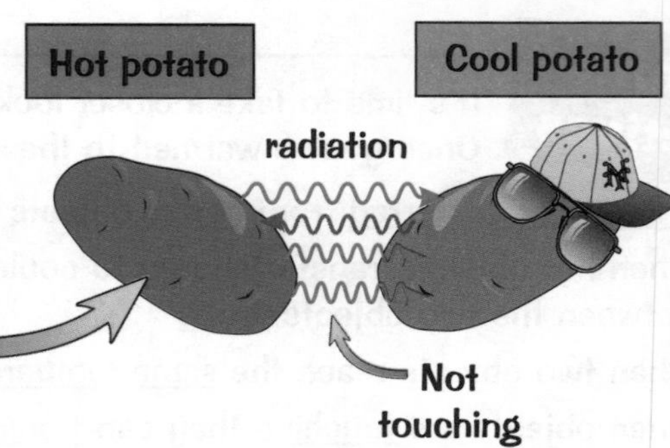

1) All objects radiate invisible waves which carry energy to their surroundings — the hotter an object is, the more energy it will radiate.
2) This radiation isn't transferred by particles, so the objects don't need to be touching.
3) The hotter object (like this hot potato) radiates more than the cooler object.
4) It emits more radiation than it absorbs, so it cools down.
5) The cooler object absorbs some of the radiation from the hot object.
6) It absorbs more radiation than it emits, so it heats up.

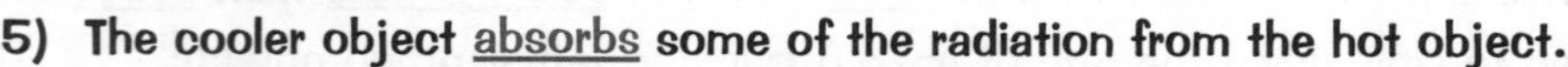

Insulators Slow Down the Rate of Energy Transfer

1) Some materials transfer energy by heating more quickly than others.
2) Materials that transfer energy by heating quickly (like metals) are called conductors. Materials that transfer energy by heating more slowly (like plastics) are called insulators.
3) Wrapping an object in an insulator will slow down the rate at which it transfers energy by heating to and from surrounding objects. So insulators help keep hot objects hot, and cold objects cold.

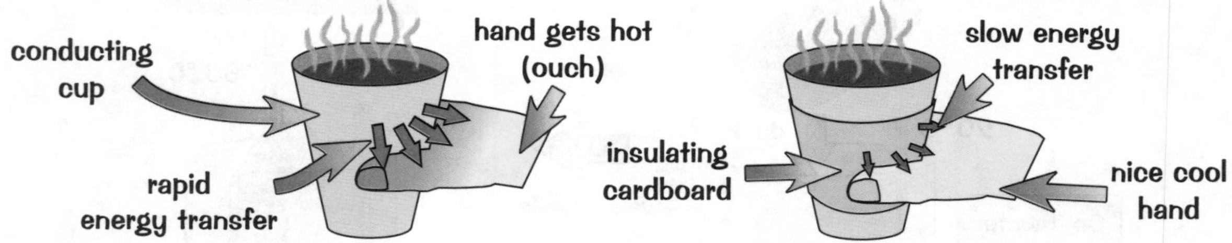

Horridly Helpful Heating Questions

Quick Fire Questions

Q1 If two objects with different temperatures are pushed together, in which direction will most energy be transferred?

Q2 What's it called when two objects reach the same temperature?

Q3 What name is given to a material that doesn't transfer energy by heating quickly?

Practice Questions

Q1 The statements below are all describing either conduction or radiation. Write the appropriate word next to each to show which of the two it is describing.

(a) For energy to transfer between two objects, they must be touching. ....

(b) In this process, energy is transferred by invisible waves. ....

(c) **All** objects transfer energy to their surroundings by this process. ....

Q2 Most of the energy in thermal energy stores on Earth comes from the Sun.

(a) Name the heating process by which energy from the Sun gets to the Earth. ....

(b) Kai says "The Earth is much cooler than the Sun, so the Earth does not transfer energy to its surroundings." Do you agree with Kai? Explain your answer.

....

....

Q3 Oliver heats one end of a piece of copper wire in a Bunsen burner flame. The other end of the wire soon gets hot as well.

(a) What heating process transfers the energy along the wire?

....

(b) Describe how the energy is transferred along the wire.

....

....

....

Q4 Jess wants to investigate which materials are best at keeping hot drinks hot. She has three cups — one metal cup, one cardboard cup and one plastic cup. She plans to fill each cup with hot water from a kettle and put lids on them. WS

plastic metal cardboard

After five minutes, Jess will use a thermometer to measure the temperature of the water in each cup.

(a) Jess chooses three cups that are the same size and shape and have walls of the same thickness. Suggest **one** other thing that she should do to make sure that her experiment is a fair test.

....

(b) Suggest **one** thing that Jess should do to make sure that her experiment is safe.

....

(c) In which cup do you expect the temperature of the water will have decreased the most after five minutes? Explain your prediction.

....

....

....

Topic Review How did you get on with the questions? Are you confident on all the learning objectives?

Conservation of Energy

Learning Objectives

If you thought energy disappears when it's not used, you'd be wrong. Turns out it's just being moved into other stores. By the end of this topic you should know...

- that energy is always conserved — it can be transferred, but not created or destroyed
- that the total energy before a transfer is always the same as the total energy after a transfer
- that the total energy before and after a transfer can be measured (in Joules).

The Principles of Conservation of Energy

Scientists have only been studying energy for about two or three hundred years so far, and in that short space of time they've already come up with two "Pretty Important Principles" relating to energy. Learn them really well:

THE PRINCIPLE OF CONSERVATION OF ENERGY

Energy can never be CREATED nor DESTROYED — it's only ever TRANSFERRED from one store to another.

That means energy never simply disappears — it's always transferred to another store. This is another very useful principle:

Energy is ONLY USEFUL when it's TRANSFERRED from one store to another.

Think about it — all useful machines use energy from one store and transfer it to another store.

For example: a stretched catapult has energy in its elastic energy store. This energy isn't useful until it's transferred to the kinetic energy store of the rock.

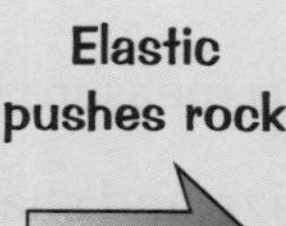

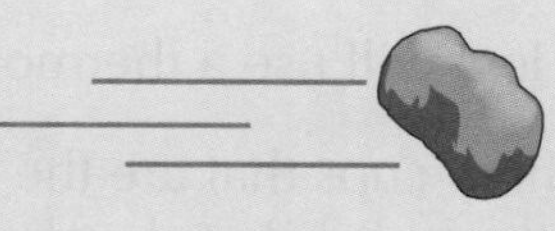

Most Energy Transfers are Not Perfect

1) Useful devices transfer energy from one store to another.
2) Some energy is always lost in some way, nearly always as by heating.
3) As the diagram shows, the energy input will always end up coming out partly as useful energy and partly as wasted energy — but no energy is destroyed:

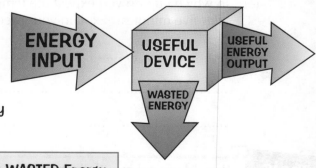

ENERGY INPUT → USEFUL DEVICE → USEFUL ENERGY OUTPUT; WASTED ENERGY

Total Energy INPUT = The USEFUL Energy + The WASTED Energy

Here's an Example

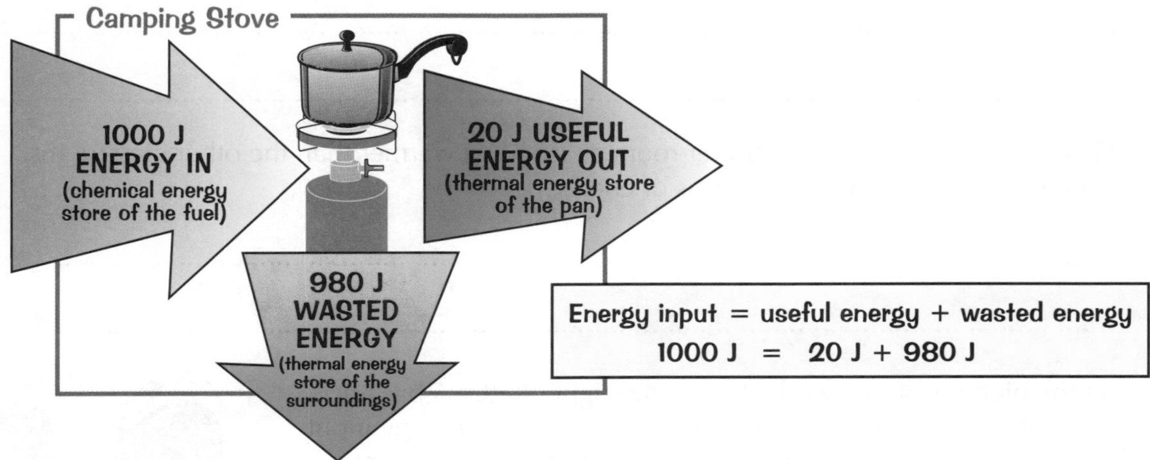

You Can Draw Energy Transfer Diagrams

1) You can show how energy moves between stores by drawing an energy transfer diagram.
2) Rectangles are used to represent the different stores.
3) Draw an arrow to show energy being transferred and label it with the method of transfer.
4) If there's more than one transfer, draw an arrow for each one, each going to a different store.

For example, for the camping stove above:

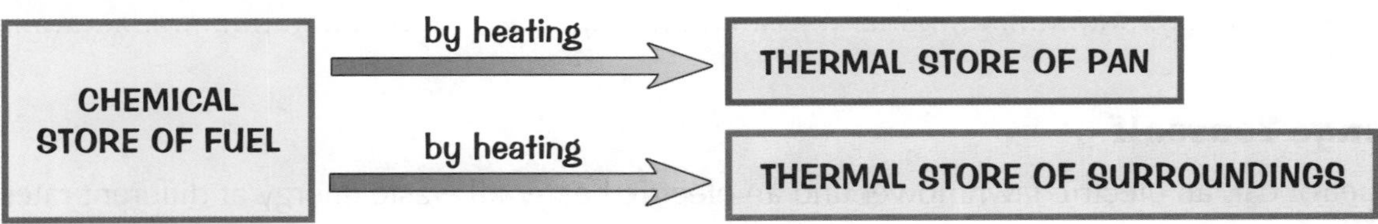

Comparably Concise Conservation of Energy Questions

Quick Fire Questions

Q1 Write down the principle of conservation of energy.

Q2 The useful energy output from a car is lower than the energy it was supplied with. What has happened to the rest of the energy?

Q3 All of the energy supplied by a battery to an electric motor is transferred to the motor's kinetic energy store and the thermal energy stores of the motor and its surroundings. If 10 kJ of energy is supplied by the battery and 4 kJ is transferred to the kinetic energy store of the motor, how much energy is transferred to thermal energy stores of the motor and the surroundings?

Practice Questions

Q1 Put a tick in the boxes next to the statements below that are **true**.

☐ Energy is only useful when it's transferred from one store to another.

☐ The useful energy output from a machine is the same as the energy input.

☐ Energy is always useful.

☐ Machines transfer input energy to useful output energy stores.

Q2 (a) Gemma says that energy can be created by rubbing two sticks together really fast. Is she correct? Explain your answer.

....

....

(b) Gemma notices that the computer room at school is warmer than the other classrooms. Explain why this might be, in terms of energy.

....

....

Q3 Look at the pictures of the two kettles on the right. Kettle A has an energy input of 1000 joules per second. Kettle B has an energy input of 2500 joules per second. Both kettles transfer the same amount of energy per second to the thermal energy store of the water they contain.

Kettle A 1000 joules

Kettle B 2500 joules

(a) Explain how it is possible that both kettles can transfer the same amount of energy to the water when they have different energy inputs.

....

(b) Suggest **two** advantages of using kettle A instead of kettle B.

1. ....

2. ....

Challenge Yourself

Q4 A petrol car, an electric lawnmower and an electric heater all waste energy at different rates.

(a) (i) For every 100 joules of energy input, the car wastes 75 joules. Find the useful energy output of the car.

Useful energy = ... joules

(ii) For every 80 joules of useful energy output, the lawnmower wastes 120 joules. Find the input energy of the lawnmower.

Input energy = ... joules

(iii) The electric heater has an energy input of 400 joules and a useful energy output of 80 joules. Find the energy wasted by the heater.

Energy wasted = ... joules

(b) What is the **useful** output energy store that energy is transferred to by:

(i) both the car and the lawnmower? ....

(ii) the electric heater? ....

Topic Review

Did you feel confident answering the questions?
Are you sure you've got all the learning objectives sussed?

Fuels and Energy Resources

Learning Objectives

The Sun's a useful little critter. It provides us with oodles of energy and asks for nothing in return. By the time you've sailed through this topic, you should know...

- what fuels are and what we use them for
- that most of our energy resources come from the Sun
- how energy from the Sun is transferred to the energy resources that we use.

We Burn Fuels for Energy

See page 7 for more on all the different stores of energy.

1) Most of the energy we use is locked up in the chemical energy stores of fuels.
2) When we burn the fuels, the energy is transferred to thermal energy stores.
3) We can transfer this energy into other useful stores, like the kinetic energy store of a car. We can also use it directly, e.g. to heat houses.
4) Fuels include biomass (see below) and fossil fuels.

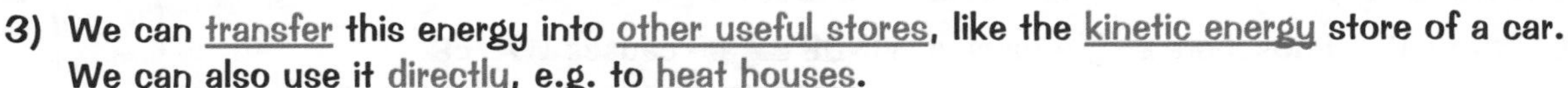

Fossil Fuels Come from Long-Dead Plants and Animals

1) Fossil fuels include coal, oil and natural gas (methane).
2) They're formed from the remains of dead plants and animals. These remains got buried under layers of mud, rock and sand millions of years ago.
3) The remains slowly decayed and turned into fossil fuels, ready for us to burn.
4) Because they take ages to form, we can't replace fossil fuels once they're burnt. That makes them non-renewable (see page 22).

The Sun is the Source of Our Energy Resources

Most of the energy around us originates from the Sun. The Sun's energy can be used to supply our energy demands — but it's often transferred to different stores before we use it.

The Sun's Energy is Transferred in Lots of Different Ways

1 *Sun's Energy ⟶ Coal, Oil, and Gas (Fossil Fuels)*

Sun ⇨ light ⇨ photosynthesis ⇨ dead plants/animals ⇨ FOSSIL FUELS

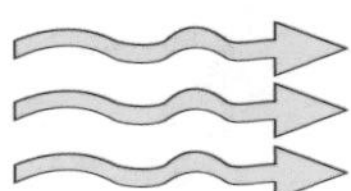

2 *Sun's Energy ⟶ Biomass (e.g. Wood)*

Sun ⇨ light ⇨ plants ⇨ photosynthesis ⇨ BIOMASS (wood)

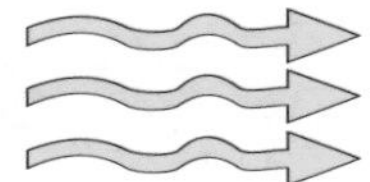

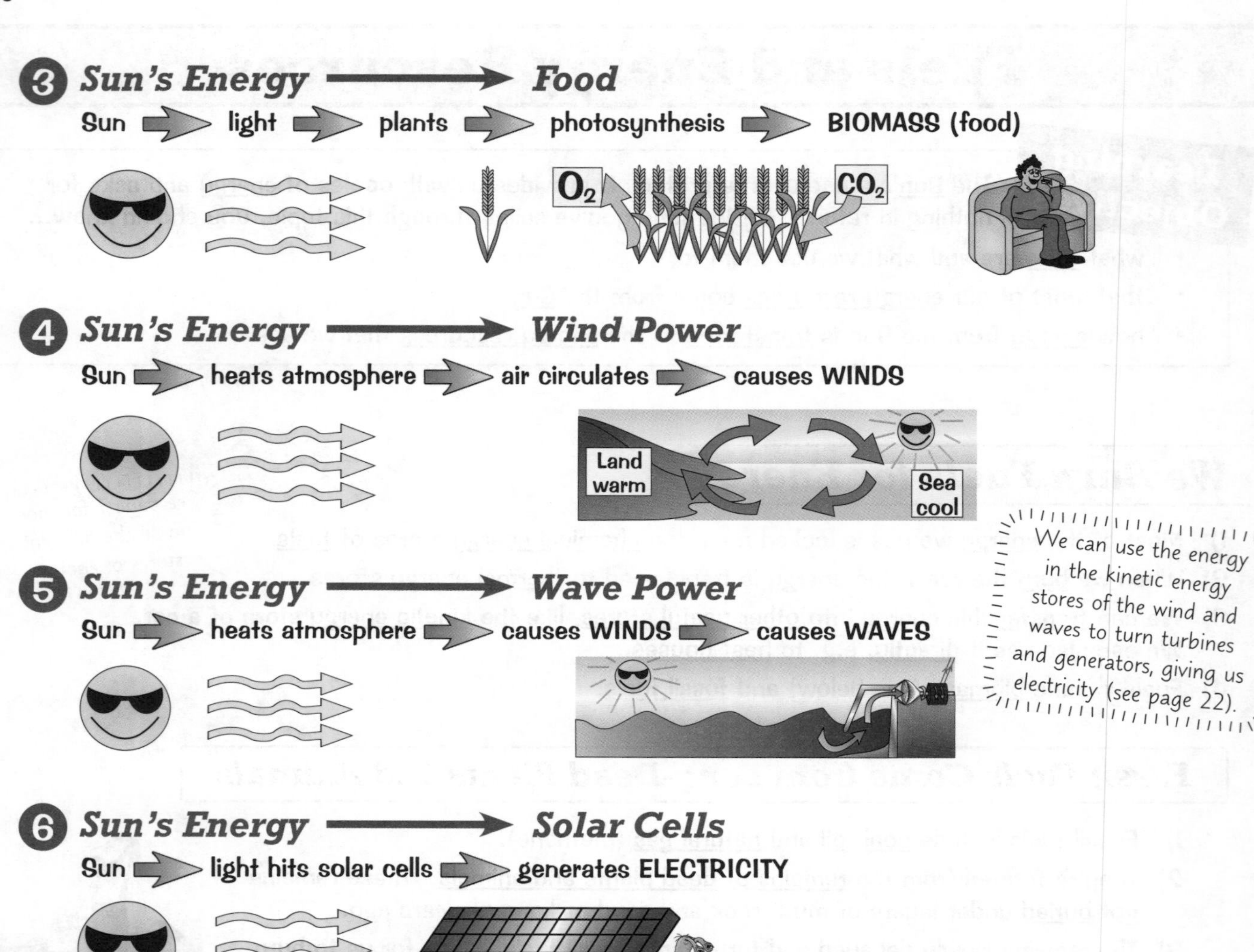

Sun ⇨ heats atmosphere ⇨ air circulates ⇨ causes WINDS

Land warm Sea cool

We can use the energy in the kinetic energy stores of the wind and waves to turn turbines and generators, giving us electricity (see page 22).

❺ Sun's Energy ⟶ Wave Power

Sun ⇨ heats atmosphere ⇨ causes WINDS ⇨ causes WAVES

❻ Sun's Energy ⟶ Solar Cells

Sun ⇨ light hits solar cells ⇨ generates ELECTRICITY

Fantastically Elegant Fuel and Energy Questions

Quick Fire Questions

Q1 How do we obtain energy from fuels?

Q2 Give two examples of fossil fuels.

Q3 Write out a chain to show how energy can be transferred from the Sun to biomass (in the form of wood).

Practice Questions

Q1 Fill in the gaps in these chains to show how energy from the Sun is transferred to different energy resources.

(a) Sun's energy to food:

Sun → light → plants → .... → biomass (food)

(b) Sun's energy to fossil fuels:

Sun → light → photosynthesis → .... → fossil fuels

(c) Sun's energy to wind power:

Sun → .... → air circulates → ....

Q2 Light from the Sun can provide us with energy resources in the form of fossil fuels and biomass.

(a) Name the process that plants use to transfer energy from light into biomass.

....

(b) (i) Describe how fossil fuels are formed.

....

....

....

(ii) Name the energy store that energy is transferred from when a fossil fuel is burnt.

....

(c) Name **two** types of biomass that we use as energy resources.

1 ....

2 ....

Q3 The diagram below shows how the Sun causes winds.

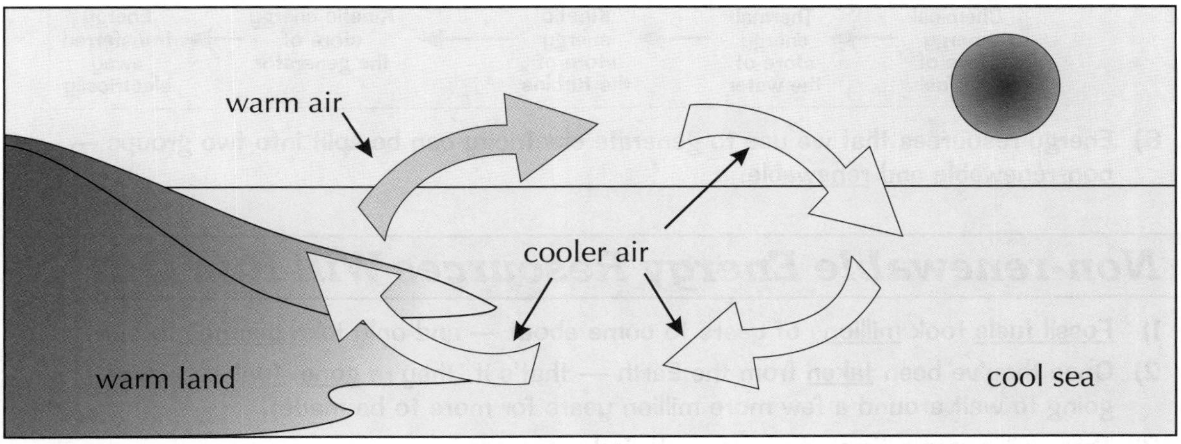

Briefly explain how the energy in the wind's kinetic energy store is used to generate electricity.

....

....

....

Topic Review

How did you get on with the questions?
Have you nailed the learning objectives?

Generating Electricity

Learning Objectives

We need electricity for pretty much everything nowadays — so it's pretty important that we make sure we're generating enough. After this topic, you should...

- know that energy resources can be used to generate electricity
- know that energy resources can be classed as renewable or non-renewable
- understand that non-renewable energy resources will eventually run out
- understand that it's important to try to conserve energy and electricity as much as possible.

There Are Different Ways of Generating Electricity

1) There are a variety of different fuels that people use in their homes, e.g. coal is used for fires, gas is used for cookers, etc. But most homes these days rely on electricity for most of their energy needs.
2) We can use energy resources (see pages 19-20) to generate electricity.
3) Most ways of generating electricity involve transferring energy to a turbine's kinetic energy store.
4) The turbine is connected to a generator, which turns with the turbine, generating electricity. The energy in the generator's kinetic energy store is transferred away electrically.
5) At the moment we generate most of our electricity by burning fossil fuels:

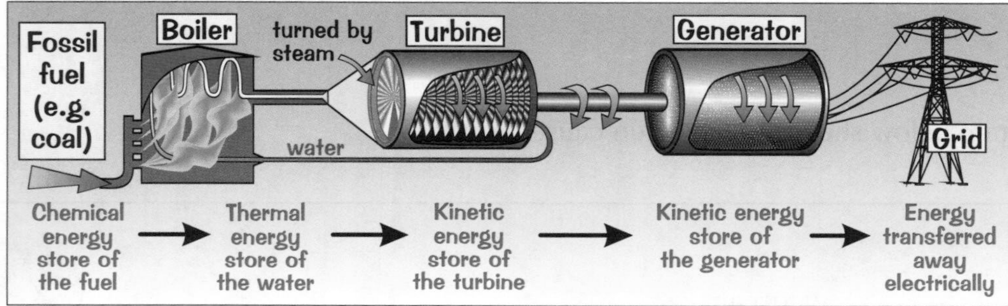

6) Energy resources that we use to generate electricity can be split into two groups — non-renewable and renewable.

Non-renewable Energy Resources Will Run Out

1) Fossil fuels took millions of years to come about — and only take minutes to burn.
2) Once they've been taken from the Earth — that's it, they're gone, (unless you're going to wait around a few more million years for more to be made).
3) There will come a time when we can't find any more.

We Need to Reduce the Amount of Fossil Fuels We Use

1) It makes sense that the quicker we use fossil fuels, the quicker they'll run out. Once this happens, it's a big problem — we'll need to find alternatives as soon as possible.
2) We need to make the fossil fuels we do have last as long as possible. We can help to do this by:

i) Saving energy (e.g. turning things off, driving cars with fuel-efficient engines).
ii) Recycling more.
iii) Using more renewable energy resources (see next page).

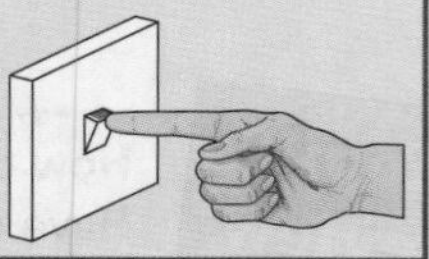

Renewable Energy Resources Won't Run Out

As long as the Sun still shines...

1. The WIND will always blow — and turn turbines and generators to make electricity.

2. PLANTS will always grow — which can be burnt to generate electricity.

3. WAVES will always be made — and drive generators to make electricity.

4. SOLAR cells will always work — and use energy transferred by light to make electricity.

Generally Joyful Questions on Generating Electricity

Quick Fire Questions

Q1 Describe what the difference is between a renewable and a non-renewable energy resource.

Q2 Why will fossil fuels eventually run out?

Practice Questions

Q1 The amount of fossil fuels burnt can be reduced by **saving energy** and by using **renewable energy resources** instead.

(a) Explain why scientists warn that we should reduce the rate at which we are burning fossil fuels.

....

....

....

(b) Give **two** examples of things you can do to help save energy.

1 ....

2 ....

(c) Name **three** renewable energy resources that could be used to help replace fossil fuels.

1 ....

2 ....

3 ....

Q2 Many calculators have a solar cell like the one in the picture.

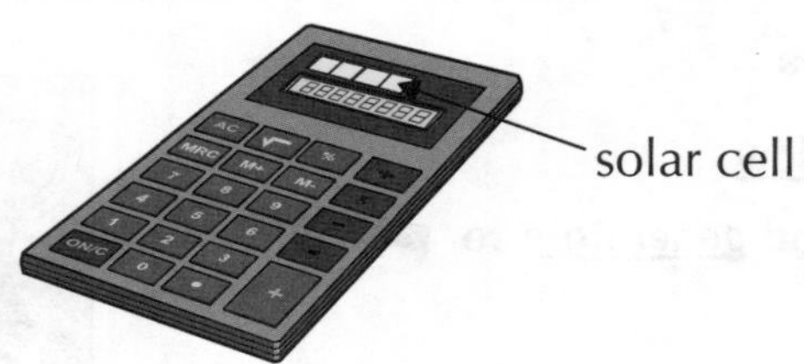

(a) Suggest **one advantage** and **one disadvantage** of using solar cells to power a calculator.

Advantage: ....

Disadvantage: ....

(b) Making a new calculator uses energy. Jay's calculator is broken, so he is going to throw it away. Suggest something else Jay could do with the calculator instead to help save energy.

....

Q3 The three main parts of a power station are shown below.

A B C

(a) Name **one** fuel that could be used in a power station like this one.

....

(b) Write down the **letters** of the parts in the order that they are used to generate electricity. Write the **name** of the part next to each letter.

1. **Letter** .... **Name** ....

2. **Letter** .... **Name** ....

3. **Letter** .... **Name** ....

(c) (i) Write the letter of the part where energy is transferred from the fuel's chemical energy store to thermal energy stores. ....

(ii) Write the letter of the part where energy from a kinetic energy store is transferred electrically. ....

Topic Review **Did you make it through the questions without a hitch? Got the learning objectives memorised?**

The Cost of Electricity

Learning Objectives

Generating electricity costs power plants money, so it's no surprise that they charge you for it. By the end of this topic you should be able to...

- use the units joules, kilojoules and kilowatt-hours to measure energy transferred
- calculate the energy transferred by an electrical appliance
- read electricity meters and compare amounts of electricity transferred
- calculate the cost of electricity used based on electricity meter readings.

You Can Calculate the Energy an Appliance Transfers

1) Anything that needs electricity to work is an electrical appliance.
2) All electrical appliances transfer energy electrically into other stores of energy. Energy can be measured in joules (J), kilojoules (kJ) or kilowatt-hours (kWh).

- Joules are the standard unit of energy — you've probably come across that one before.
- A kilojoule is just a thousand joules. It's used when a lot of energy's being transferred, so you don't have to use really big numbers all the time.
- Kilowatt-hours are used in domestic fuel bills because they're easier to keep track of — 1 kWh is the energy you'd use if you left a 1 kW appliance on for 1 hour. Simple. Just remember, a kWh is a unit of energy, not power or time.

3) Power tells you how fast something transfers energy. It's usually measured in watts (W) or kilowatts (kW). 1 kW = 1000 W.
4) The total amount of energy transferred by an appliance depends on the amount of time that it's switched on for and its power.
5) If you know the power in watts and the time in seconds, you can calculate energy transferred using this equation:

ENERGY TRANSFERRED (J) = POWER (W) × TIME (s)

EXAMPLE: Calculate the energy transferred, in joules, by a 2 kW appliance left on for 30 minutes.

ANSWER: 2 kW = 2000 W 30 minutes = 30 × 60 = 1800 seconds
Energy transferred = 2000 × 1800 = 3 600 000 J

6) If you know the power in kilowatts and the time in hours, you can use this equation:

ENERGY TRANSFERRED (kWh) = POWER (kW) × TIME (h)

EXAMPLE: Calculate the energy transferred, in kWh, by a 2 kW appliance left on for 30 minutes.

ANSWER: 30 minutes = 0.5 hours
Energy transferred = 2 × 0.5 = 1 kWh

This is another good reason for using kWh in fuel bills — saying you've used 1 kWh is much easier than saying you've used 3 600 000 J.

Electricity Meters **Record** *How Much Energy* **is Used**

Electricity meters record the amount of energy transferred in kWh. You can use them to work out the energy transferred over different periods of time, e.g. at day and at night:

EXAMPLE: Govinda wants to find out how much electricity he uses during the day compared to during the night. He writes down his meter reading at three different times during a 24 hour period:

4 4 2 8 1 . 2 5 kWh

Day 1, 6 p.m. 44281.25 kWh   Day 2, 6 a.m. 44284.76 kWh   Day 2, 6 p.m. 44296.12 kWh

Does he use more electricity during the day or during the night?

ANSWER: Energy from 6 p.m. to 6 a.m. (during the night) = 44284.76 – 44281.25 = 3.51 kWh
Energy from 6 a.m. to 6 p.m. (during the day) = 44296.12 – 44284.76 = 11.36 kWh
So he uses more electricity during the day.

Calculating the *Cost of Electricity*

Domestic fuel bills charge by the kilowatt-hour.
You can calculate what your electricity bill should be using this handy little formula:

COST = Energy transferred (kWh) × PRICE per kWh

Cost = kWh × Price

EXAMPLE: Electricity costs 16p per kWh. At the start of last month, Jo's electricity meter reading was 42729.66 kWh. At the end of the month it was 43044.91 kWh. Calculate the cost of her electricity bill last month.

ANSWER: Energy transferred = final meter reading – initial meter reading
= 43044.91 – 42729.66 = 315.25 kWh
Cost in pence = Energy transferred (kWh) × price per kWh (p)
= 315.25 × 16 = 5044p
Cost in pounds = 5044 ÷ 100 = £50.44

Many homes use gas as a fuel, e.g. for gas central heating, gas cookers etc.
Your gas bill is calculated using the energy transferred in kWh, just like your electricity bill.

Comfortingly Quaint Cost of Electricity Questions

Quick Fire Questions

Q1 Write down two formulas, with units, you could use to find the energy transferred by an appliance.

Q2 What does an electricity meter measure?

Practice Questions

Q1 Use the words below to complete these sentences.

kWh   energy   kilowatt   power   hours   time   hour

(a) The .... transferred by an appliance in kWh depends on its .... in kilowatts and the .... in .... that it is on for.

(b) One .... is the amount of energy transferred by an appliance with a power of one .... used for a time of one ....

Q2 A 40 W appliance is left on for 2 hours.

(a) Calculate the energy, in J, that the appliance transfers during this time.

Energy = ... J

(b) Calculate the energy, in kWh, that the appliance transfers during this time.

Energy = ... kWh

Q3 Sandrine wants to know whether she uses more electricity in her home or in her office. She reads the electricity meter for each on Monday morning, and then again on Sunday evening.

	Home	Office
Monday	27431.65 kWh	61844.95 kWh
Sunday	27604.15 kWh	61974.45 kWh

(a) Does she use more electricity at home or in the office over the course of a week?

She uses more electricity ....

(b) If electricity costs 10 p per kWh, calculate Sandrine's electricity bill for the week at home and in the office.

Cost at home = £ .... Cost in the office = £ ....

Challenge Yourself

Q4 A student's room has a TV (300 W), heater (1000 W) and a lamp (100 W). Electricity costs 10p per kWh.

Calculate how much it would cost to run these three appliances for a total of 2 hours 30 minutes.

Cost = ... p

Topic Review

Did you sail through the questions without any trouble?
Are you sure you understand all of the learning objectives?

Comparing Power Ratings and Energy Values

Learning Objectives

You might not look that similar to a toaster, but your body and an electrical appliance both need energy to work. Once you've powered through this topic, you should...

- know that the power rating of an appliance tells you how much energy it transfers in a given time
- be able to compare the energy transferred by different appliances by looking at their power rating
- know that the label on foods tells you how much energy that food provides
- be able to compare the energy provided by different foods by looking at their labels.

Power Ratings of Appliances

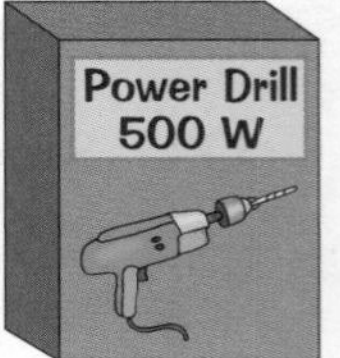

1) The power rating of an appliance is the energy that it transfers per second when it's operating at its recommended maximum power (i.e. when it's plugged into the mains).
2) You can work out the energy transferred by an appliance in a certain time if you know its power rating. To do this you need to use the equations on page 25.

The *Energy Transferred* Depends on the *Power Rating*

1) The higher the power rating of an appliance, the more energy it transfers in a given amount of time.
2) You can compare how much energy is transferred by appliances with different power ratings.

EXAMPLE: How much energy is transferred by a 1.5 kW electric heater compared to a 4 kW electric heater, when they're both left on for 1.5 hours?

ANSWER: Energy transferred (kWh) = power rating (kW) × time (h).
Energy transferred by the 1.5 kW heater = 1.5 × 1.5 = 2.25 kWh.
Energy transferred by the 4 kW heater = 4 × 1.5 = 6 kWh.

So the 4 kW heater transfers (6 – 2.25) 3.75 kWh more energy than the 1.5 kW heater in 1.5 hours.

3) Remember, transferring energy costs money. So an appliance with a higher power rating will cost more to run over a set period of time than an appliance with a lower power rating. In the example above, the 4 kW heater would cost more to run for an hour and a half than the 1.5 kW heater.

Food Labels Tell You *How Much Energy* is in Food

1) All the food we eat contains energy — it's important to make sure you're taking in the right amount of energy each day.
2) The energy in food is measured in kilojoules (kJ).
3) You can compare the amount of energy in different foods by looking at their labels.

You might also see values for kcals on food labels — this is just another unit that energy can be measured in.

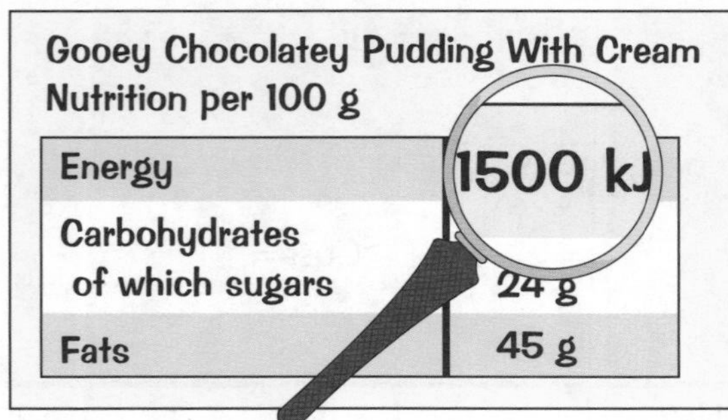

Gooey Chocolatey Pudding With Cream
Nutrition per 100 g

Energy	1500 kJ
Carbohydrates of which sugars	 24 g
Fats	45 g

Super Healthy Nutritious Fruit Salad
Nutrition per 100 g

Energy	150 kJ
Carbohydrates of which sugars	 9 g
Fats	0 g

These labels tell you that the chocolate pudding has ten times more energy stored in it than the fruit salad.

Politely Plucky Power and Energy Questions

Quick Fire Questions

Q1 Which will transfer more energy: a 2 kW heater left on for 1 hour, or a 200 W TV left on for 1 hour?

Q2 Which contains more energy: a 450 kJ bar of chocolate or an 800 kJ stick of butter?

Practice Questions

Q1 Use the words below to complete these sentences.

power **kilojoules** **second** **maximum** **energy** **labels**

(a) The .... rating of an appliance, in watts, is the .... that it transfers per .... when it's operating at its recommended .... power.

(b) Energy in foods is measured in .... (or kcals). You can compare the amount of energy found in different foods by looking at their ....

Q2 Harrison is investigating the energy content of two different brands of crisps.
The top of the label for each bag of crisps is shown below.

Runners Salty Shack Share Bag 55 g Nutritional values per bag	
Energy	1260 kJ
Fat	15 g
Carbohydrates	27 g

McBain's Crumplies 35 g Nutritional values per bag	
Energy	960 kJ
Fat	13 g
Carbohydrates	18 g

Harrison empties each bag onto a heat-proof mat and places a beaker of cold water on a tripod above the crisps. He then sets fire to the crisps and measures how much the temperature of the water rises once all the crisps have burned.

(a) Which bag of crisps do you expect to heat a beaker of water the most? Explain your answer.

....

....

(b) Harrison's friend suggests that the test is not a fair comparison of the two crisps. Suggest why.

....

Challenge Yourself

Q3 Evelyn has an electric heater with a power rating of 1 kW and another with a power rating of 2.5 kW. She works out that she can afford to keep the 2.5 kW heater running for 1.5 hours each evening. How long could she afford to run the 1 kW heater instead?

Time = ... hours

Topic Review

How did you get on with the questions?
Do you feel like you could ace a surprise test on this topic?

Physical Changes

Learning Objectives

A substance can change physically without any chemical reaction happening — like ice melting into water. When you've worked through this topic, you should...

- know that a physical change doesn't involve a change in mass
- understand how physical changes are different to chemical changes
- know that melting, evaporating, condensing, freezing, sublimation and dissolving don't involve a change in the amount of a substance present
- know that all of these physical changes are reversible
- understand how a change of state affects a substance's physical properties
- know that ice is unusual because it becomes more dense when it melts (into water).

Physical Changes Don't Involve a Change in Mass

1) A substance can either be a solid, a liquid or a gas. These are called states of matter.
2) When a substance changes between these physical states, its mass doesn't change.
3) Physical changes are different to chemical changes because there's no actual reaction taking place and no new substances are made. The particles stay the same, they just have a different arrangement and amount of energy.

There are several different processes that can change the physical state of a substance:

Melting, Evaporating, Condensing, Freezing

1) If you melt a certain amount of ice, you get the same amount of water — and then if you boil that so it evaporates, you get the same amount of steam.
2) It's the same in the other direction — if the steam condenses, you get the same amount of water, and if the water freezes, you get the same amount of ice.

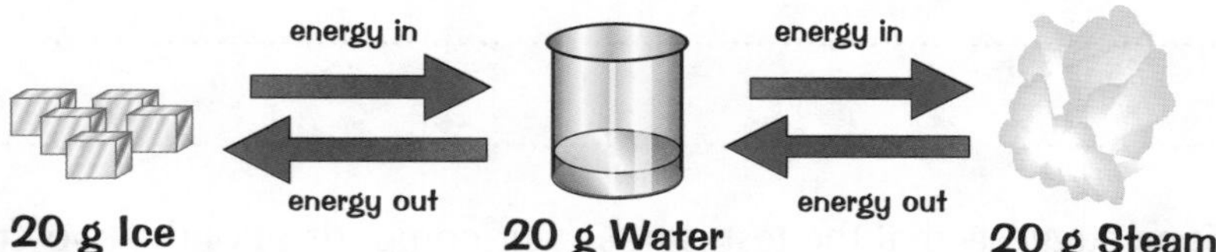

3) These reactions are all reversible — if water freezes, just heat it up and it'll melt back into water.

Sublimation

Some substances, such as carbon dioxide, can go straight from being a solid to being a gas — this is called sublimation. When this happens, the mass of gas is (you guessed it) the same as the mass of the solid.

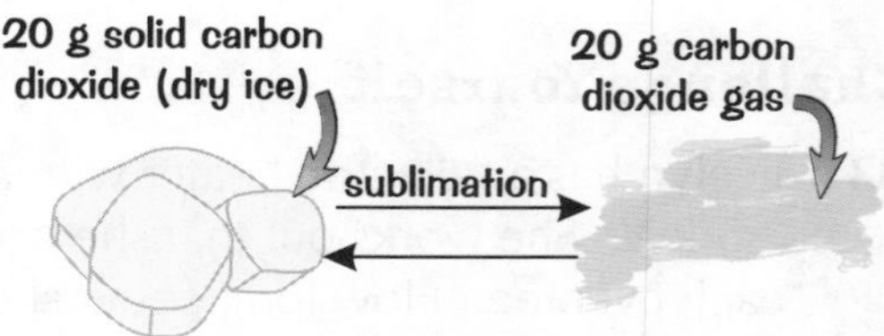

Dissolving

1) When a solid substance dissolves to form a solution, there's no change in mass. The amount of substance after dissolving is the same as before, it's just in a different form.
2) Dissolving is reversible — if you evaporate all the solvent, you'll be left with the same amount of solid as before it dissolved.

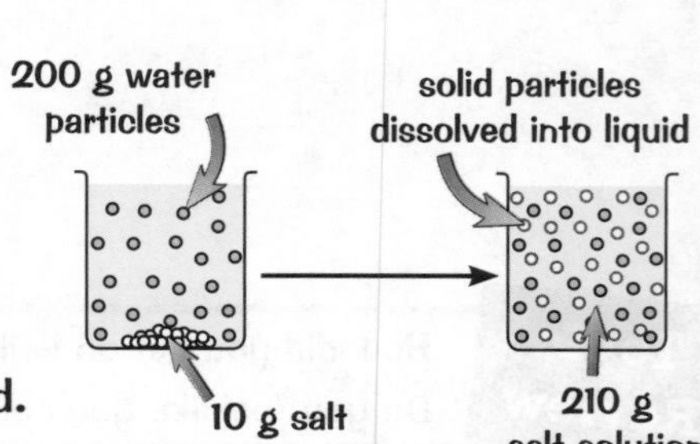

Changes of State Affect a Substance's Physical Properties

1) The particles in solids are packed together tightly compared to gases and liquids — so they're usually more dense. They're also difficult to compress and can't flow.
2) The particles in liquids and gases are free to move around each other, so they can flow.

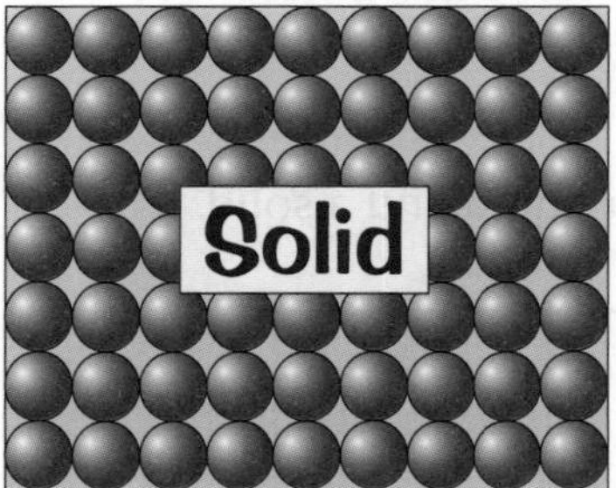

Particles are packed tightly and cannot move around. Substance is dense and difficult to compress.

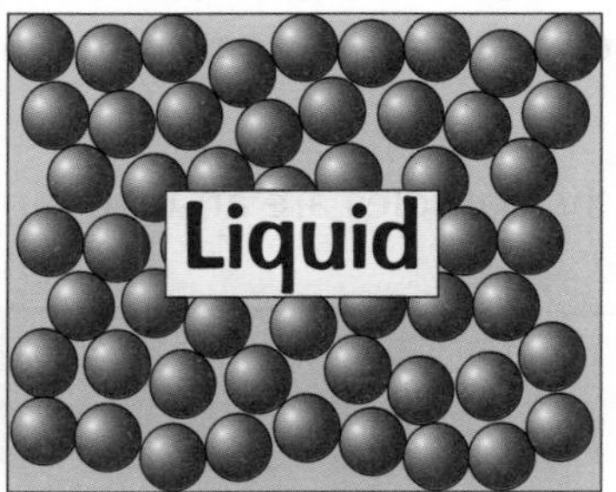

Particles are fairly close together, but can move around. Substance is fairly dense and difficult to compress.

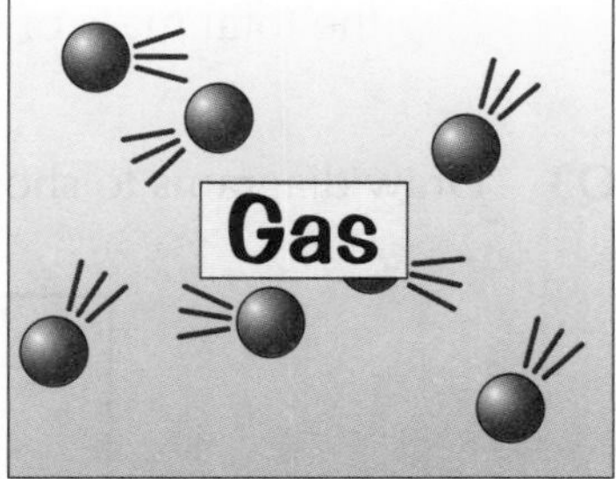

Particles are very far apart and can move around easily. Substance is not very dense, and easy to compress.

3) When you heat a substance, the particles move around more and move further apart, causing it to change from a solid, to a liquid, to a gas. The substance expands and becomes less dense.

Ice Becomes More Dense When it Melts

1) Ice is a funny one though — when it melts (to become water), the particles actually come closer together and its density increases.
2) That's why ice floats on water. It seems normal because water is so common, but you'd usually expect a solid to sink in a pool of its liquid form.

Frightfully Fantastic Physical Changes Questions

Quick Fire Questions

Q1 What's the difference between a physical change and a chemical change?

Q2 What's it called when a substance changes straight from a solid to a gas?

Q3 In which state of matter are the particles most free to move around?

Q4 When a gas condenses into a liquid does it become more dense or less dense?

Practice Questions

Q1 Draw lines to match each description below to the correct state of matter.

Easy to compress.	**Solid**
Particles are packed together tightly.	**Liquid**
Particles are fairly close together but free to move around.	**Gas**

Q2 Complete these sentences by crossing out the incorrect word(s) in each set of brackets.

(a) A change of state, like a liquid becoming a gas, is (**reversible / irreversible**).

(b) When a physical change happens, the particles present at the end are (**different to / the same as**) the particles present at the start.

(c) The total mass of substances before a physical change is (**the same as / different to**) the total mass of substances after a physical change.

Q3 Draw diagrams to show how the particles are arranged in a gas, a liquid and a solid.

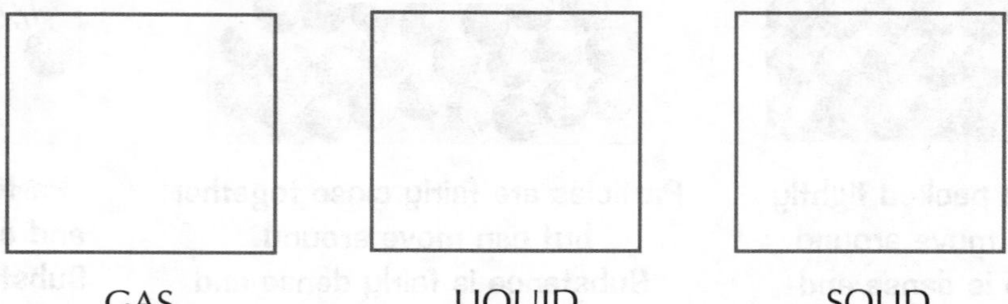

Q4 Sara wants to find the melting point of tin. She uses a Bunsen burner to heat a 10 g sample of tin until it melts. Sara measures the temperature of the tin with a temperature probe.

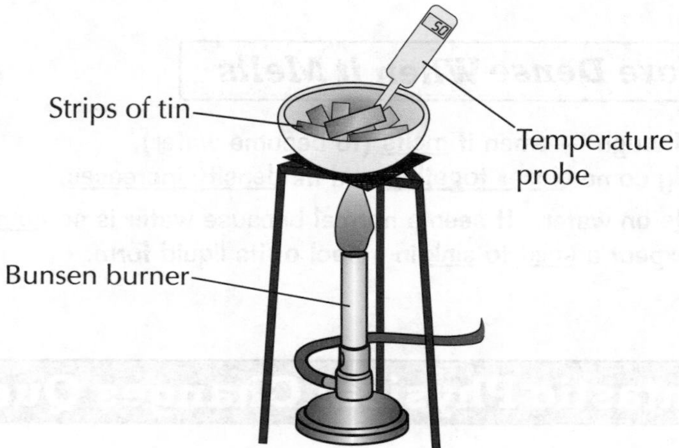

(a) Suggest **one** safety precaution Sara should take when conducting this experiment.

....

(b) State what mass of melted tin Sara would have at the end of the experiment. ....

(c) (i) What would Sara expect to happen to the density of the tin as it melts?

....

(ii) Would the same be true if Sara had been heating ice? Explain your answer.

....

....

Topic Review **Did you feel confident answering the questions?**
Are you sure you've got all the learning objectives sussed?

Movement of Particles

Learning Objectives

The particles that make up all matter are constantly wiggling and jiggling around. By the time you've wriggled through this topic, you should...

- know that Brownian motion is the random movement of tiny particles, like atoms and molecules, in liquids and gases
- understand that the random motion of particles causes substances to diffuse from areas of high concentration to areas of low concentration
- know that increasing the temperature of a substance causes its particles to move around more
- know that increasing the temperature of a substance increases the space between its particles.

Brownian Motion is the *Random Movement* of Particles

1) In 1827, a scientist called Robert Brown noticed that tiny pollen particles moved with a zigzag, random motion in water.
2) This type of movement of any particle suspended ('floating') within a liquid or gas is known as Brownian motion.

Atoms and molecules are both types of particle.

3) Large, heavy particles (e.g. smoke) can be moved with Brownian motion by smaller, lighter particles (e.g. air) travelling at high speeds. The particles collide, sending each other off in random directions.

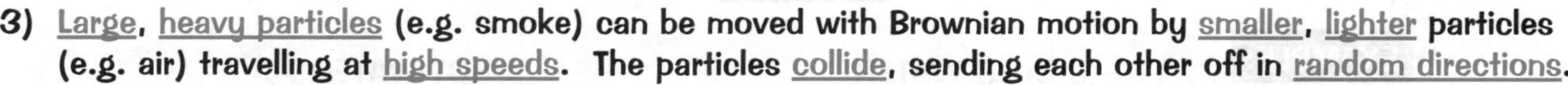

4) This is why smoke particles in air appear to move around randomly when you observe them in the lab.

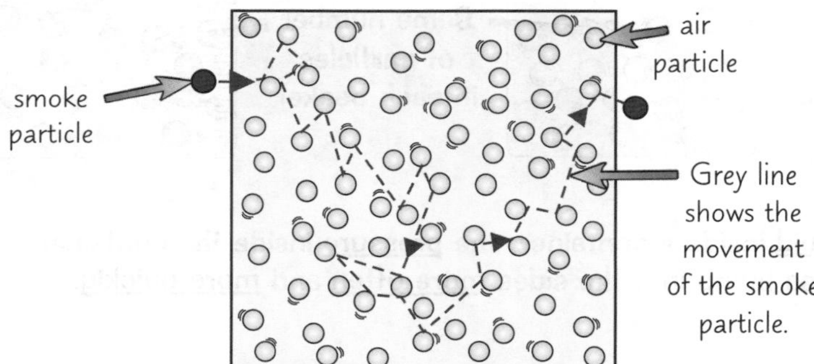
air particle
smoke particle
Grey line shows the movement of the smoke particle.

Diffusion is Caused by *Random Movement* of Particles

1) Diffusion is when a substance moves from an area of high concentration (where there's lots of it) to an area of low concentration (where there's less of it).
2) It happens because the particles in a liquid or gas move around at random.
3) They constantly bump into each other and bounce around until they're evenly spread out.

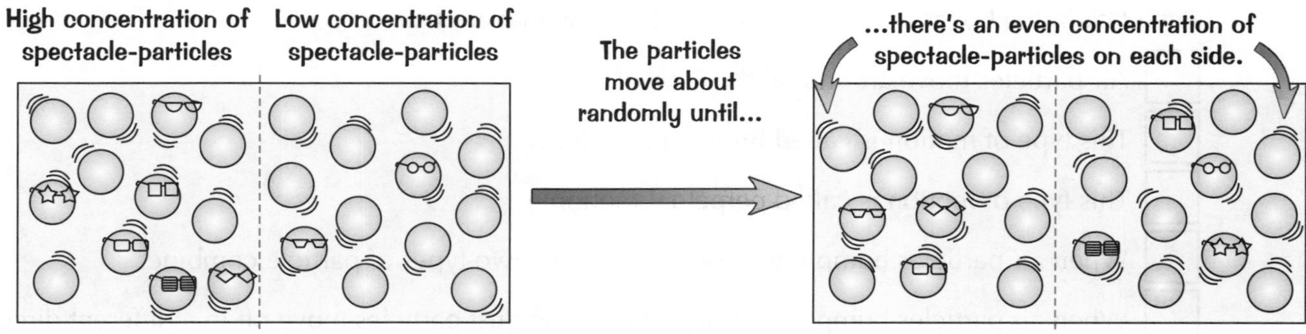
High concentration of spectacle-particles
Low concentration of spectacle-particles
The particles move about randomly until...
...there's an even concentration of spectacle-particles on each side.

Movement of Particles Increases With Temperature

1) An increase in temperature causes particles to move around more — their speed increases.
2) This means that the spaces between the particles get bigger so they take up more space.
3) So heating a solid, a liquid or a gas will make it expand.

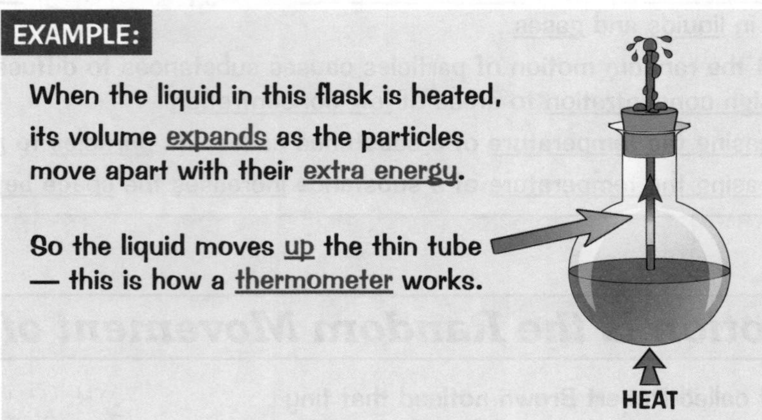

EXAMPLE:
When the liquid in this flask is heated, its volume expands as the particles move apart with their extra energy.
So the liquid moves up the thin tube — this is how a thermometer works.
HEAT

4) The number of particles doesn't change and the particles don't get bigger — the particles that are there just need more space to move around in.

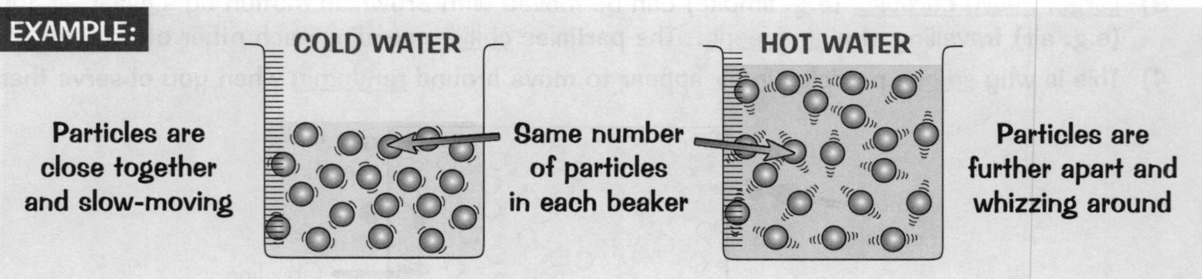

5) If you heat a gas or liquid inside a container, the pressure inside the container increases as the particles bump into the sides more often and more quickly.

Positively Peachy Particle Movement Questions

Quick Fire Questions

Q1 What is diffusion?

Q2 What effect does temperature have on the movement of particles?

Practice Questions

Q1 In a brightly lit room, you can sometimes see dust particles moving around in the air. Put a tick in the boxes next to the statements below that are **true**.

- [ ] Air particles move around all the time.
- [ ] This type of motion is called Brownian motion.
- [ ] This type of motion is called perpetual motion.
- [ ] When air particles bump into dust particles, the two types of particle combine.
- [ ] When air particles bump into dust particles, the dust particles move off in a different direction.

Q2 Sasha sprays some air freshener. After a few minutes Chesney can smell it at the other end of the corridor. Complete the sentences by using the words below:

spread **particles** **lots** **few** **diffusion**

To start with, there are .... of smell particles where Sasha is.

Gradually, they .... out. The smell .... have moved from where there are lots of them to where there are only a .... of them.

This process is called ....

Q3 Draw out what the particles in a solid might look like before heating and after heating (but not enough to melt it). Use circles to represent the particles.

BEFORE AFTER

Q4 A round-bottomed flask full of air was warmed with warm hands and the tube coming out of it was placed into some blue liquid. After a few moments, bubbles could be seen coming from the tube. The flask was clamped and allowed to return back to room temperature. Soon, blue liquid could be seen creeping up the tube.

(a) Does warm air take up more or less volume than cold air?

....

(b) Explain why bubbles could be seen coming from the tube as the flask was warmed.

....

....

....

(c) Explain why the blue liquid crept up the tube as the flask cooled.

....

....

....

Topic Review How did you get on with the questions? Have you nailed the learning objectives?

Speed

Learning Objectives

Speed is all about how fast things are moving — but don't zoom through these pages at 100 mph. By the time you reach the end, you'll be able to:

- understand the relationship between speed, distance and time
- use the formula speed = distance ÷ time.

Speed is How Fast You're Going

1) Speed is a measure of how far you travel in a set amount of time.
2) This is the formula that you use for calculating speed:

$$\text{Speed} = \frac{\text{Distance}}{\text{Time}}$$

This line means divided by or shared by (÷).

You can use the word SIDOT to help you remember the formula.

SIDOT — Speed Is Distance Over Time.

3) Always remember to include the units in any speed calculation that you do. There are three common units for speed:

- metres per second — m/s
- miles per hour — mph or miles/h
- kilometres per hour — km/h

You should realise that they're all kind of the same, i.e. distance unit per time unit.

4) The best way to do speed calculations is to use a formula triangle.

Formula Triangles are Like Equation Cheat Sheets

1) A formula triangle makes it easy to rearrange a formula so that you can calculate the thing that you want. They're incredibly handy.
2) All you need to do is cover up the letter you want to calculate with your thumb. Then the triangle tells you what you need to do:

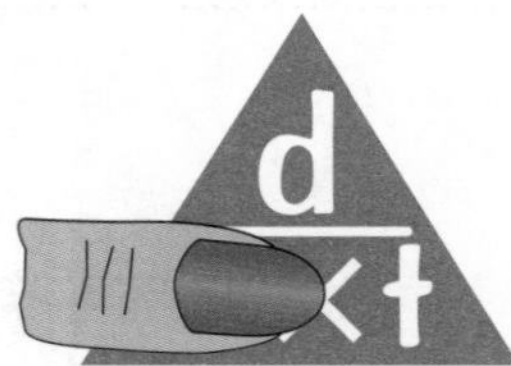

1) To calculate speed, cover up the s. This leaves you with $\frac{d}{t}$.
2) The horizontal line means divided by or shared by.
3) So speed = distance ÷ time.

1) To calculate distance travelled, cover up the d. This leaves you with s × t.
2) So distance = speed × time.

1) To calculate time taken, cover up the t. This leaves you with $\frac{d}{s}$.
2) The horizontal line means divided by or shared by.
3) So time = distance ÷ speed.

Use the Formula to Work Out Speed, Distance or Time

Example 1:

A hooligan sheep is skateboarding down a farmer's track.
You notice it takes exactly 5 seconds to move between two fence posts, 10 metres apart. What's the sheep's speed?

Answer:

STEP 1) Write down what you know:
distance, d = 10 m   time, t = 5 s

STEP 2) We want to find speed, s. From the formula triangle: s=d/t
Speed = Distance ÷ Time = 10 ÷ 5 = 2 m/s

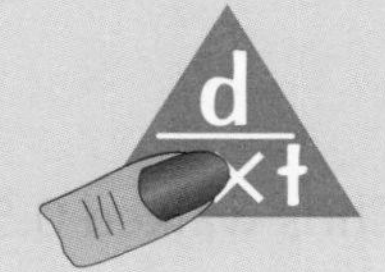

Remember to make sure that all the numbers are in the RIGHT UNITS before you put them in the formula.

Example 2:

A camper van trundles down the road, travelling 15 miles in 30 minutes. What's its speed in miles per hour?

Answer:

STEP 1) Write down what you know and put the units into miles and hours:
distance, d = 15 miles   time, t = 30 minutes = 0.5 of an hour.

STEP 2) We want to find speed, s. From the formula triangle: s=d/t
Speed = Distance ÷ Time = 15 ÷ 0.5 = 30 miles/hour (mph)

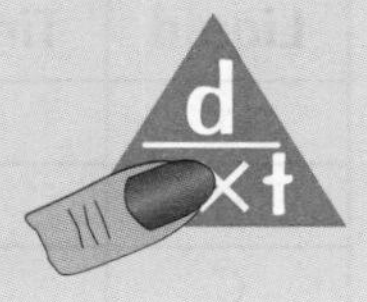

Example 3:

A cyclist cycles at 33 kilometres per hour for a quarter of an hour. How far does the cyclist travel?

Answer:

STEP 1) Write down what you know:
speed, s = 33 kilometres per hour   time, t = 0.25 of an hour.

STEP 2) We want to find distance, d. From the formula triangle: d = s × t
Distance = Speed × Time = 33 × 0.25 = 8.25 km

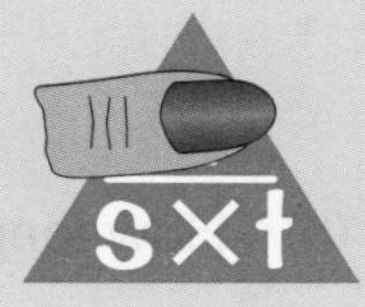

Splendidly Spiffing Speed Questions

Quick Fire Questions

Q1 Write down the formula for speed.

Q2 Name three units that you could use to measure speed.

Practice Questions

Q1 A racehorse ran 402 m in 22.8 s. Find his speed in m/s.

Answer: .... m/s

Q2 Bernard the snail moved 38 cm in 140 s. Work out his speed in cm/s.

Answer: .... cm/s

Q3 Chris and Jenny both walked to the same beach, but they took different routes.

(a) Jenny took 15 minutes to reach the beach and walked 700 m to get there.
What speed was she travelling at, in km/hour? Show your working.

Answer: .... km/h

(b) Chris walked 0.5 km to the beach at 0.1 km/min. How long did it take him to get to the beach?

Answer: .... minutes

Q4 A scientist is investigating the properties of various liquids.
He drops a metal ball down a tube filled with one of the liquids and measures how long it takes for the ball to pass between two marks on the tube.
The marks are 50 cm apart. The table below shows some of his results.

WS

Liquid	Time for ball to pass between marks	Speed
A	10 seconds	
B	2 seconds	
C	5 seconds	
D		1.0 m/s
E		2.5 m/s
F		0.4 m/s

tube
liquid
metal ball
50 cm
stopwatch
00:00

(a) What was the speed of the ball in liquid C, in metres per second?

Answer: .... m/s

(b) How long did the ball take to pass between the marks in liquid D in seconds?

Answer: .... s

(c) How long, in seconds, would the ball take to pass through 15 m of liquid E?

Answer: .... s

(d) How far, in metres, through liquid F would the ball travel in 23 seconds?

Answer: .... m

Topic Review

How did you find the questions?
Are you happy with the learning objectives?

More on Speed

Learning Objectives

There's more to speed than just calculating it (see pages 36-37).
By the time you've got these pages sussed, you'll be ace at...

- reading and plotting journeys on distance-time graphs
- working out the relative motion of two objects moving towards or away from each other.

Distance-Time **Graphs**

A distance-time graph shows the distance travelled by an object over time.
The slope of the line (gradient) shows the speed at which the object is moving:

1) The steeper the graph, the faster the object is going.
2) Flat sections are where it's stopped.
3) Downhill sections mean it's moving back toward its starting point.
4) Curves represent a changing speed.

- A steepening curve means the object is speeding up (accelerating).
- A curve levelling off means the object is slowing down (decelerating).

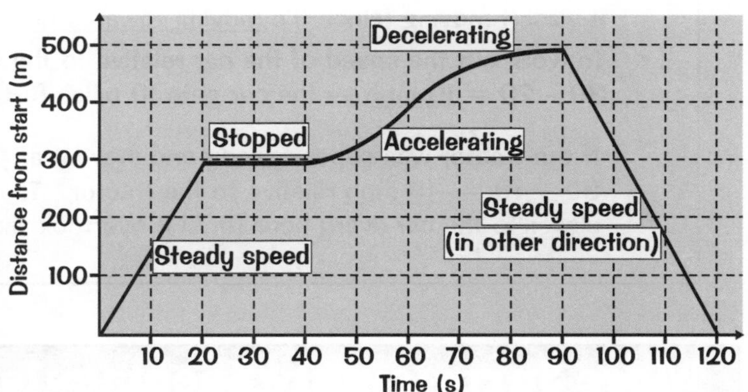

Relative Motion **is the Speed of Two** *Moving Objects*

Relative motion is useful if you want to know the speed of something when you are moving too.

1) When two objects are moving, it can be useful to know how fast they are moving together or apart — their relative motion.
2) For example, when you're travelling at 60 mph in a coach on the motorway, and a car overtakes you at 70 mph, the speed of the car is 10 mph relative to your coach. If you look out the window, the car moves past you as quickly as if you were stationary and the car was travelling at 10 mph.

Add **the** *Speeds* **of** *Two* **Objects** *Moving Towards* **Each Other**

If two objects are moving in opposite directions on the same straight line you can add their speeds together to calculate their relative motion. Look:

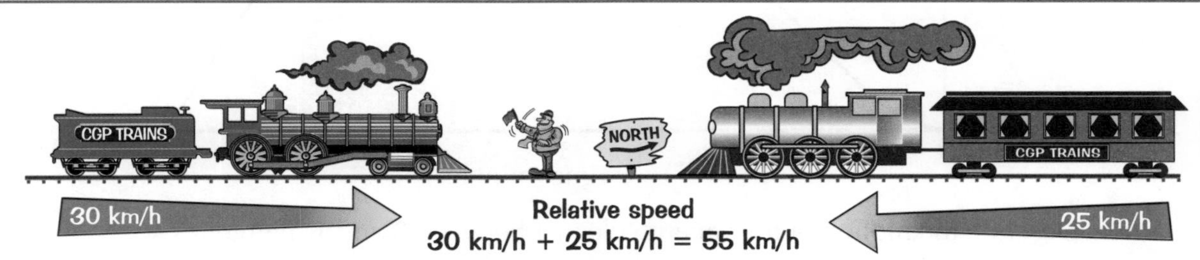

- Both trains are moving towards each other from opposite directions. So if you're sat on the red train, the blue train is getting closer much faster than if you were sat still at the side of the track. This is because it is moving towards you while you're moving towards it.
- To work out the speed of the blue train relative to the red train, just add the speeds together. 30 + 25 = 55 km/h, so the speed of the blue train relative to the red train is 55 km/h.

Subtract the Speeds of Two Objects Travelling in the Same Direction

If the objects are moving in the same direction on the same straight line you can subtract their speeds to calculate their relative motion.

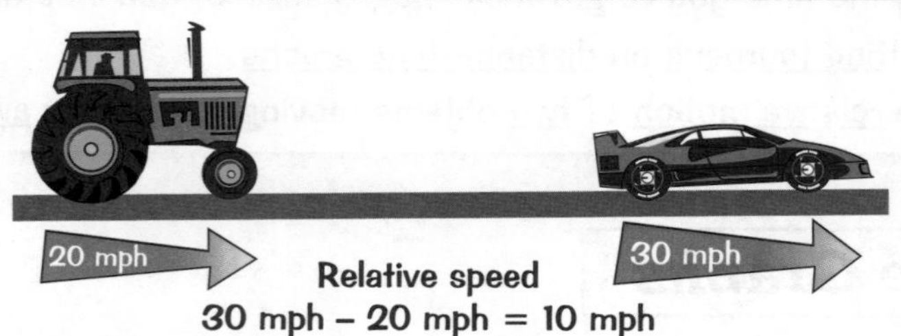

Relative speed
30 mph – 20 mph = 10 mph

- The car is moving in the same direction as the tractor but at a faster speed. If you're in the car, you're getting further away from the tractor more slowly than if it wasn't moving (since it's moving towards you while you're moving away from it).
- To work out the speed of the car relative to the tractor, subtract the speeds. 30 – 20 = 10 mph — the car gets 10 miles further away from the tractor every hour.

If the tractor was super-speedy and moving at 40 mph, the car would be moving at 30 – 40 = –10 mph relative to the tractor. That means the tractor would get 10 miles closer to the car every hour (until it overtook the car and cruised off into the distance).

More Surprisingly Spectacular Speed Questions

Quick Fire Questions

Q1 What does acceleration look like on a distance-time graph?

Q2 A car and a van are driving towards each other.
How would you calculate the speed of the van relative to the car?

Q3 A cyclist and a walker are travelling in the same direction.
How would you calculate the speed of the cyclist relative to the walker?

Practice Questions

Q1 The graph below shows the distance of a robot vacuum cleaner from its charger against time.

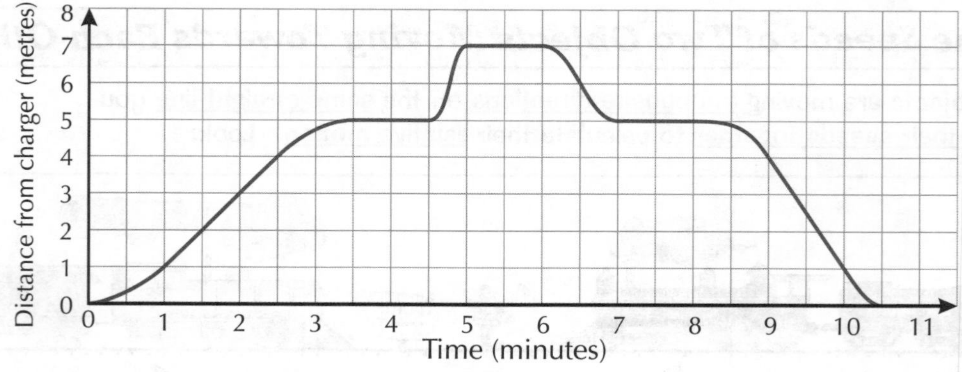

(a) Describe the motion of the vacuum cleaner between 0 and 1 minute.

....

(b) Calculate the speed of the cleaner between 9 and 10 minutes in metres per second.

Answer: .... m/s

(c) In which direction is the vacuum cleaner moving between 9 and 10 minutes?

....

(d) Circle two periods on the graph where the vacuum cleaner is not moving.

(e) Draw an arrow pointing to the part of the graph where the vacuum cleaner was moving fastest.

Q2 The diagram below shows two trains that are moving towards each other on separate tracks.

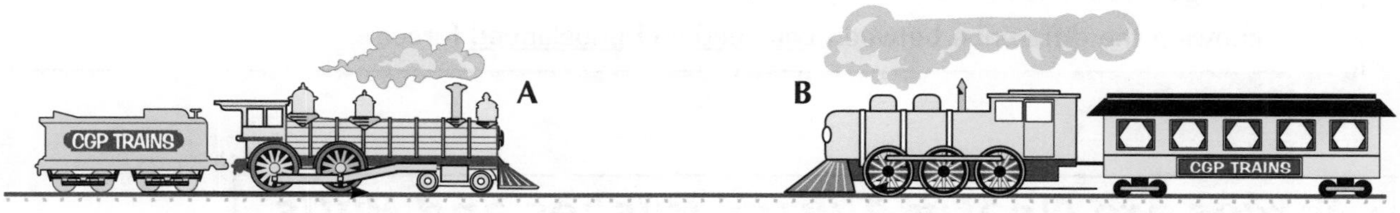

A B
CGP TRAINS CGP TRAINS
30 mph 45 mph

What is the speed of train B relative to train A?

Answer: .... mph

Q3 A car is overtaking a school bus on a motorway.

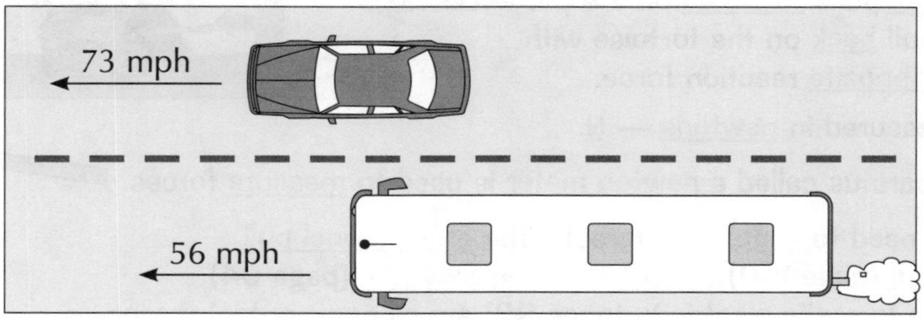

73 mph
56 mph

(a) Calculate the speed of the car relative to the bus.

Answer: .... mph

Challenge Yourself

(b) The bus and the car both pull into a service station 25 miles after the car overtook the bus. How many minutes sooner does the car arrive than the bus?

Answer: .... minutes

Topic Review How did you get on with the questions? Are you confident on the learning objectives?

Forces and Movement

Learning Objectives

Movement is all about forces, whether you want to start, stop or simply change direction. If you learn these pages really well, no one will be able to stop you from...

- understanding that forces are usually pushes and pulls between two objects
- knowing that forces are measured in newtons
- knowing that forces can make objects speed up, slow down, change direction, turn or change shape
- knowing the difference between balanced and unbalanced forces.

Forces are Nearly Always Pushes and Pulls

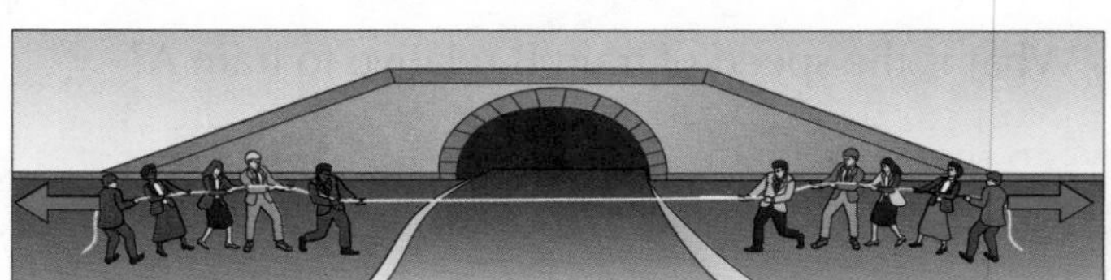

1) Forces are pushes or pulls that occur when two objects interact.
2) Forces can't be seen, but the effects of a force can be seen.
3) They always act in a certain direction.
4) Forces always act in pairs that oppose each other — an action and a reaction. E.g. if a tortoise pulls forwards on a rope, the rope will pull back on the tortoise with an equal and opposite reaction force.
5) Forces are measured in newtons — N.
6) A piece of apparatus called a newton meter is used to measure forces.
7) Objects don't need to touch to interact. The gravitational pull between planets (page 100), forces between magnets (page 94) and forces due to static electricity (page 92) are all non-contact forces.

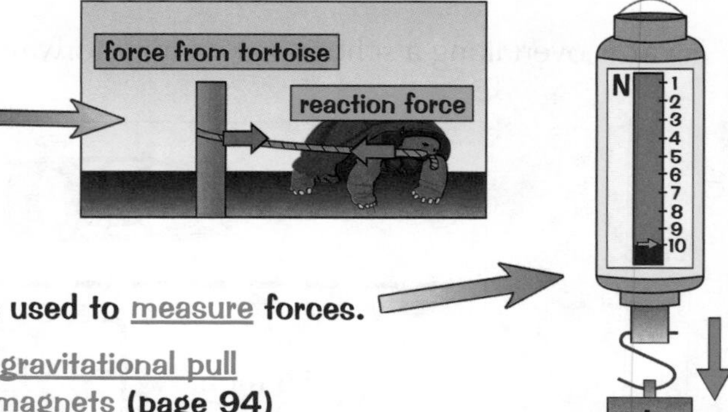

Forces Can Make Objects Do Five Things

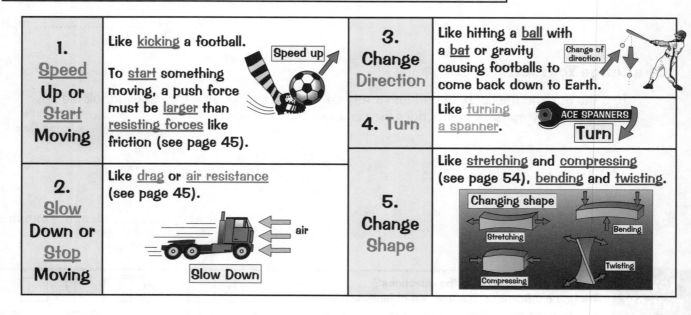

1. Speed Up or Start Moving	Like kicking a football. To start something moving, a push force must be larger than resisting forces like friction (see page 45).
2. Slow Down or Stop Moving	Like drag or air resistance (see page 45).
3. Change Direction	Like hitting a ball with a bat or gravity causing footballs to come back down to Earth.
4. Turn	Like turning a spanner.
5. Change Shape	Like stretching and compressing (see page 54), bending and twisting.

Learn These Two Important Statements:

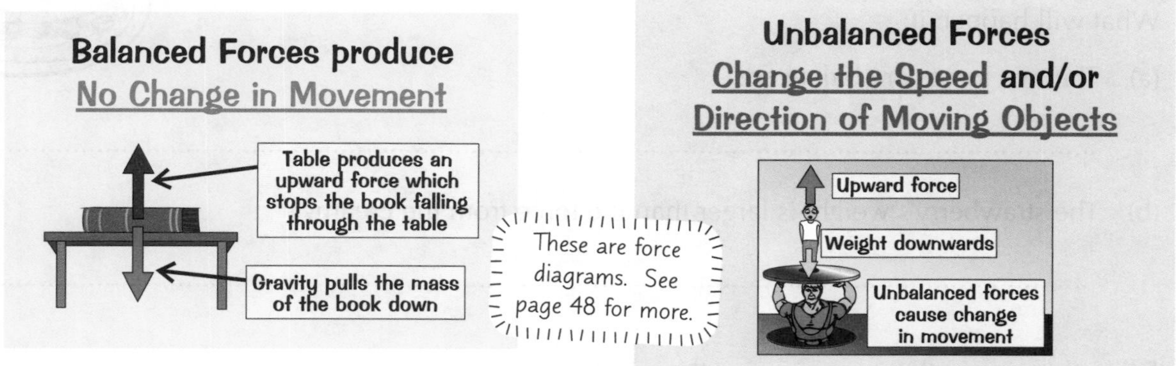
Balanced Forces produce
No Change in Movement
Table produces an upward force which stops the book falling through the table
Gravity pulls the mass of the book down
These are force diagrams. See page 48 for more.
Unbalanced Forces
Change the Speed and/or
Direction of Moving Objects
Upward force
Weight downwards
Unbalanced forces cause change in movement

1) When the arrows are the same length, the forces are balanced.
2) A pair of balanced forces cancel each other out, so there is no acceleration or change in movement. E.g. when the book is resting on the table, the upward force from the table equals the force due to gravity pulling it down, so the book does not accelerate.
3) When the arrows are different lengths, the forces are unbalanced.
4) A pair of unbalanced forces cause an acceleration or change in movement. E.g. when the bodybuilder pushes on the manhole cover, the upward force of his push is greater than the weight of the boy, so the boy accelerates upwards (as does the manhole cover).

Phenomenally Fabulous Force Questions

Quick Fire Questions

Q1 What are forces?

Q2 What unit are forces measured in?

Q3 List five things that forces can make objects do.

Q4 What is the difference between balanced and unbalanced forces?

Practice Questions

Q1 Each picture below shows a situation where a force is acting on an object. Next to each one, write down the **main** overall effect of the forces on movement. Choose from the following options:

speed up **slow down** **change direction** **change shape**

(a) A cyclist starts pedalling.

....

(b) The parachute on a drag racing car opens.

....

(c) A cricketer hits a ball that has been bowled to him.

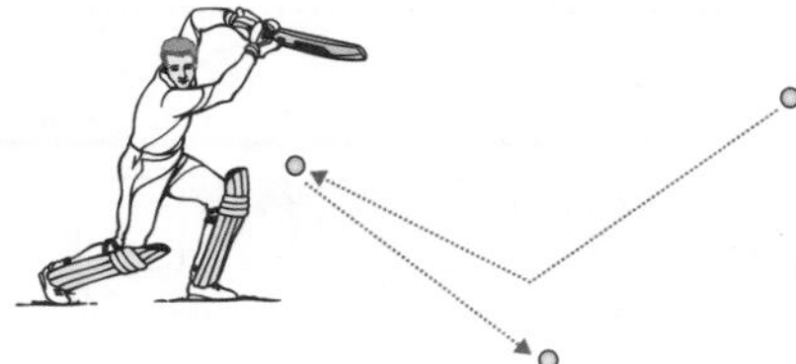

....

Q2 To finish off her cheesecake, Tessa adds a layer of whipped cream and a strawberry on top. There are two forces acting on the strawberry — an upward force from the cream and the downward force of the strawberry's weight. What will happen if:

(a) The two forces are balanced?

....

(b) The strawberry's weight is larger than the force from the cream?

....

Q3 Fill in the gaps in the passage using the words below.

non-contact reaction magnets gravitational
oppose effects pairs static

Forces act in .... that .... each other — an action force and a .... force.

Forces can't be seen, but the .... of a force can be seen.

Objects don't always need to touch to interact. The .... pull between planets, forces between .... and forces due to .... electricity are all .... forces.

Q4 For the events below write down whether the forces are BALANCED or UNBALANCED.

(a) A vase standing on a shelf.

....

(b) A cyclist starting off.

....

(c) A car slowing down.

....

(d) A ski jumper accelerating down the slope.

....

(e) A marathon runner going at a steady speed along a straight road.

....

Topic Review

Did you feel confident answering the questions?
Are you sure you've got all the learning objectives sussed?

Friction and Resistance

Learning Objectives

Friction and air resistance are forces that act against movement. They're always trying to slow you down. After these pages, you'll know all about...

- how friction tries to stop objects from sliding past each other
- air resistance and water resistance and how they affect objects moving through air and water.

Friction Tries to Stop Objects Sliding Past Each Other

Friction is a force that always acts in the opposite direction to movement.
It's the force you need to overcome when pushing an object out of the way.

The Good Side of Friction — It Allows Things to Start and Stop

1) Friction allows the tyres on a bike to grip the road surface — without this grip you couldn't make the bike move forward and you wouldn't be able to stop it either — it'd be like riding on ice.
2) Friction also acts at the brakes where they rub on the rim of the wheel or on the brake disc. Friction also lets you grip the bike — important if you want to ride it without slipping off.

The Bad Side of Friction — It Slows You Down

1) Friction always wastes energy — friction between the moving parts of a bike warms up the gears and bearings — a waste of energy.
2) Friction limits top speed. At high speed, air resistance (a kind of friction, see below) takes up most of your energy and limits your maximum speed.

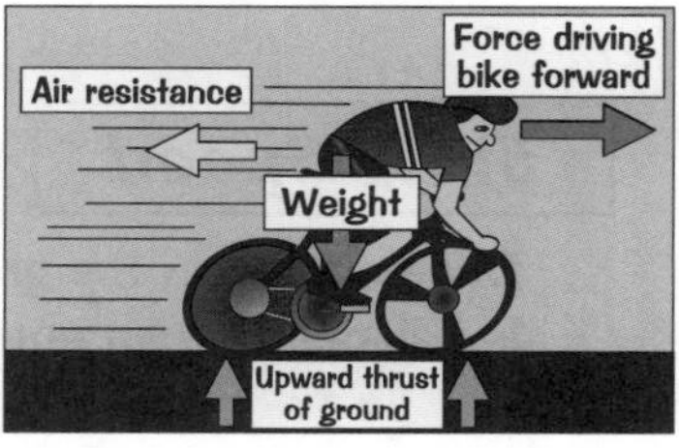

Air and Water Resistance Slow Down Moving Objects

1) Air and water resistance (or "drag") push against objects which are moving through the air or water.
2) It's because air and water have mass, and must be pushed out of the way by moving objects.
3) These are kinds of frictional force because they try to slow objects down.
4) If things need to go fast, then they have to be made very streamlined — which just means that they have a shape which can slip through the air or water without too much resistance.

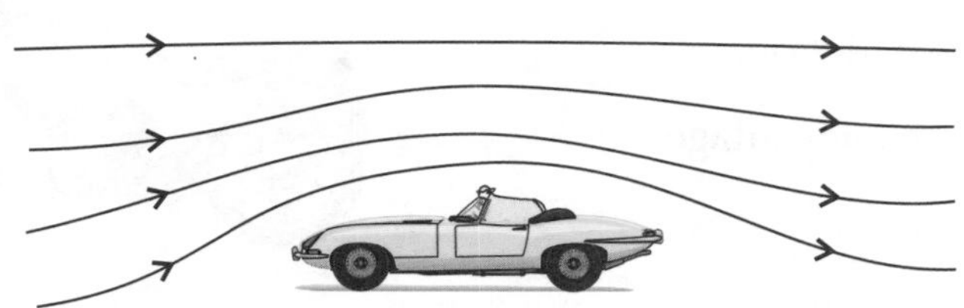

The sports car is small and smoothly shaped so air can easily flow over it. The air resistance is low.

The lorry is big and boxy. It has to punch lots of air out of the way to move forwards, so air resistance is high.

5) The same principles apply to water resistance.
Ships and submarines need to be streamlined to avoid being slowed down too much.

How Air Resistance Affects Sheep Jumping Out of Planes

(It happens all the time round here.)

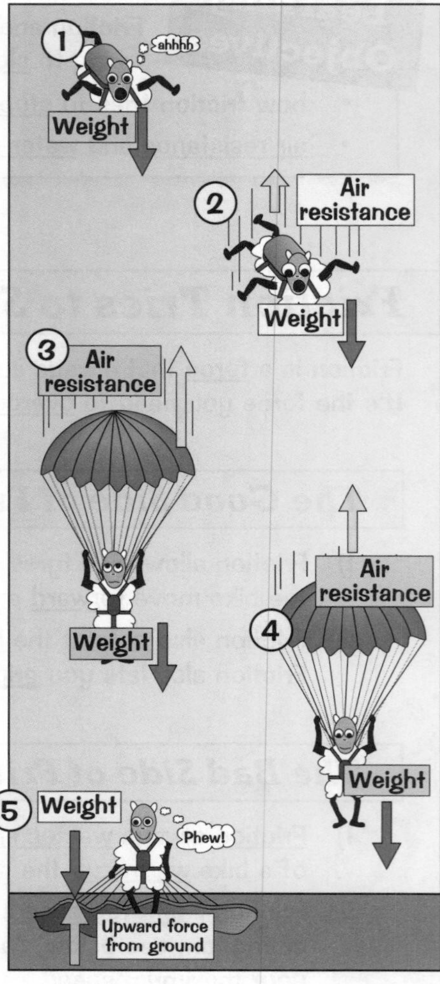

1) Gains Speed

At the start, the sheep only has the force of its weight (i.e. gravity) pulling it down — so it starts to move faster.

2) Still Gaining Speed

As it moves faster, the opposing force of air resistance gets more and more.

3) Losing Speed

When the parachute opens air resistance increases enormously — because there's a much larger area trying to cut through the air. The sheep loses speed and slows down gratefully.

4) Steady Speed

Very quickly the air resistance becomes equal to the weight — the two forces are balanced. The overall force is zero, so the sheep now moves downwards at a steady speed.

5) No Speed

Once safely on the ground, the sheep's weight acting downwards is balanced by an equal upward force from the ground.

Rather Rocking Resistance Questions

Quick Fire Questions

Q1 Complete this sentence: Friction always acts in the .... direction to movement.

Q2 Why do objects moving through air or water feel resistance?

Q3 Why does a sheep jumping out of a plane slow down when it opens its parachute?

Practice Questions

Q1 A motorbike has a smooth shape to minimise friction.

(a) Describe **two** ways in which friction is an **advantage** when riding a motorbike.

1. ....

....

2. ....

....

(b) Describe **two** ways in which friction is a **disadvantage** when riding a motorbike.

1. ....

....

2. ....

....

(c) State the technical term for a shape designed to minimise friction, like the motorbike shown.

....

Q2 A skydiver falling through the air has opposing forces acting on him due to gravity and air resistance.

(a) What is air resistance?

....

(b) (i) What happens to the skydiver when he first steps out of the plane? Explain your answer.

....

....

(ii) The skydiver starts to fall more and more quickly.
Describe what happens to the air resistance acting on him.

....

(c) (i) What happens to air resistance when the skydiver's parachute opens?

....

(ii) Explain why the skydiver falls at a steady speed with the parachute open.

....

....

(d) Explain why the skydiver stops moving once he has landed on the ground.

....

Topic Review

How did you get on with the questions?
Have you nailed the learning objectives?

Force Diagrams

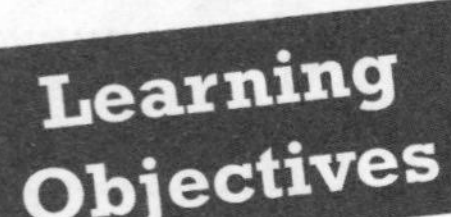

Force diagrams are a great way of working out whether the forces acting on an object are balanced. So once you've read these pages, you'll be ace at...

- showing forces as arrows in diagrams
- working out whether forces are balanced or unbalanced
- adding up forces that act along the same line.

Show the Forces Acting on an Object Using a Force Diagram

Force diagrams show the forces acting on an object and whether they are balanced or unbalanced.

Example: Stationary Teapot Force Diagram

Here's a teapot on a table...

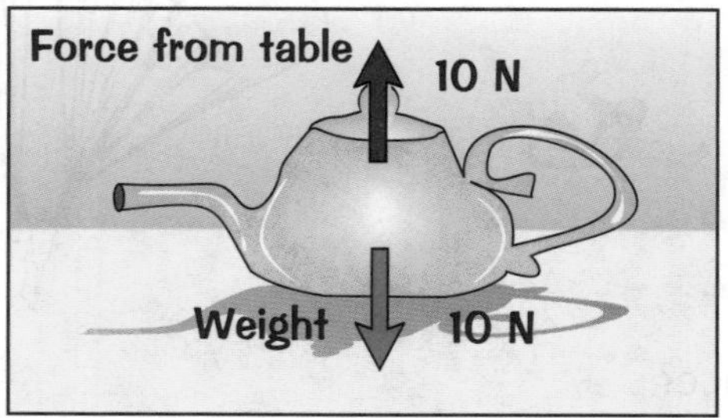

1) The force of gravity (or weight) is acting downwards on the teapot — it's the red arrow.
2) This causes a force from the table's surface pushing up on the teapot — the blue arrow.
3) The force from the table and the weight are equal and opposite — you can tell because the arrows are the same size and pointing in opposite directions.
4) This means the forces on the teapot are BALANCED. So it remains stationary (not moving).

If the teapot was moving and the forces acting on it were balanced, it would carry on moving at a steady speed in the same direction.

Example: Accelerating Bus Force Diagram

Here's a force diagram of a bus...

1) The red arrow shows that the engine is creating a force of 2000 N to make the bus move forwards.
2) The blue arrow shows that there is a frictional force of 500 N acting in the opposite direction.
3) The forces are UNBALANCED (the arrows in the diagram are unequal sizes) so the bus is accelerating in the direction of the bigger force (forwards).

If the bus was standing still (stationary) and the forces acting on it were unbalanced, it would start to move.

You Can Add or Subtract Forces Along the Same Line

1) If you've got a force diagram where all the forces are acting along the same line (e.g. forwards and backwards OR up and down), you can calculate the overall force by adding or subtracting the forces.

Forces acting along the same line are said to be acting in one dimension.

Golden Rules of Force Diagrams:

1) If the forces are acting in opposite directions, you subtract the forces to get the overall force.
2) If they're acting in the same direction, you add the forces together to get the overall force.

2) This is handy for working out if an object is accelerating (getting faster), decelerating (slowing down) or staying at a steady speed:

ACCELERATING

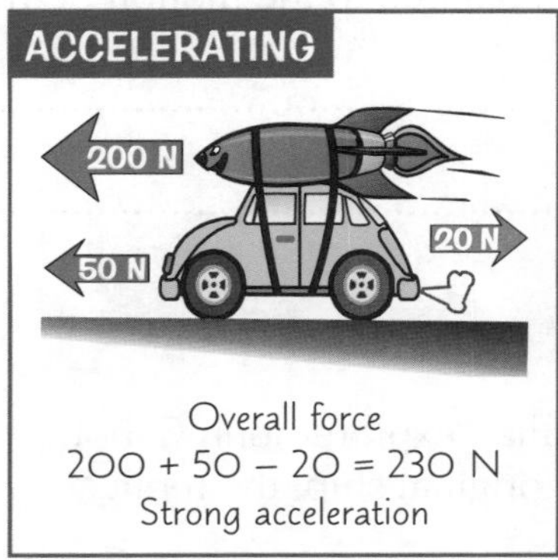

Overall force
200 + 50 − 20 = 230 N
Strong acceleration

DECELERATING

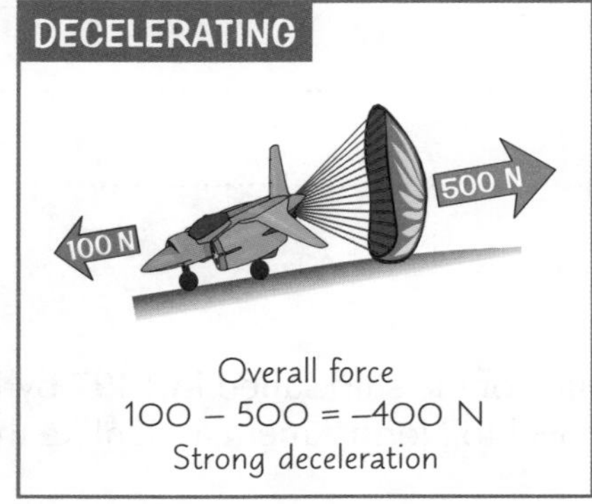

Overall force
100 − 500 = −400 N
Strong deceleration

STEADY SPEED

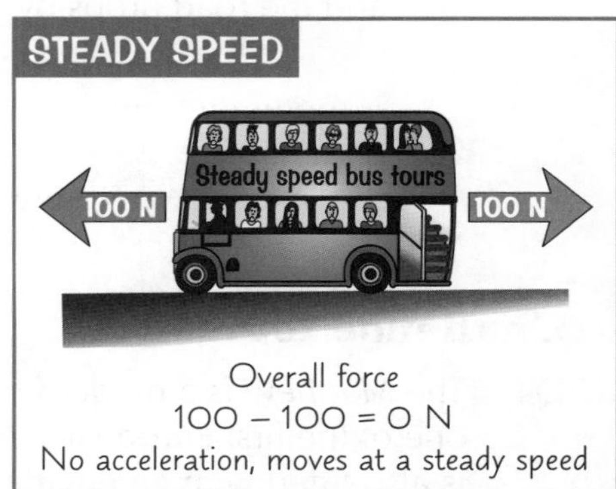

Overall force
100 − 100 = 0 N
No acceleration, moves at a steady speed

Fiercely Fortifying Force Diagram Questions

Quick Fire Questions

Q1 If the forces acting on a stationary object are unbalanced, what will happen to the object?

Q2 If the forces acting on a moving object are balanced, what will happen to the object?

Q3 When should you subtract the force arrows in a force diagram?

Q4 When should you add the force arrows in a force diagram?

Practice Questions

Q1 The diagrams below show a mass hanging from an elastic bungee rope after it has been dropped. The force of gravity acts downwards on the mass, and a force from the rope acts upwards. The upward force varies depending on the length of the rope.

A

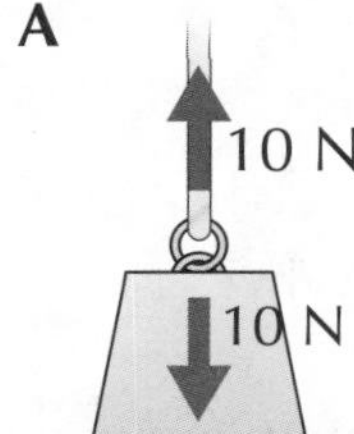

B

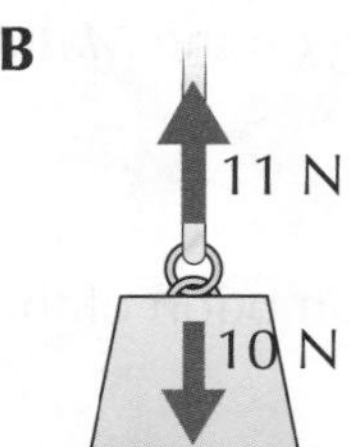

C

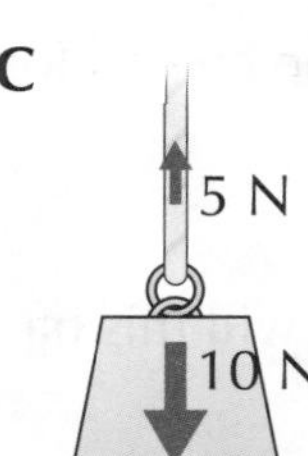

Which diagram, A, B or C, shows the mass when it is

(a) speeding up on the way down? ....

(b) speeding up on the way up? ....

(c) moving at a steady speed? ....

Q2 The diagram on the right shows a mug resting on a table.
The force from the table is 0.5 N. What is the weight of the mug?

0.5 N

....

Q3 The force diagram below shows a car travelling along a road at a steady speed.
The arrow pointing left represents the frictional force that is acting on the car.

400 N

(a) Draw the missing arrow representing the driving force on the diagram.

(b) The surface of the road that the car is travelling on changes and the friction between the tyres and the road drops by 75 N. Describe and explain what will happen to the motion of the car.

....

....

Challenge Yourself

Q4 The *Matthew* is a modern replica of the ship sailed in 1497 by Italian explorer John Cabot, one of the first Europeans to travel to North America. Unlike the original ship, the replica is also fitted with an engine.

During a voyage, the wind turns suddenly and the ship finds itself heading into the wind and the current. The diagram below shows the ship using its engine to travel forwards.

Wind and air resistance
4000 N

Driving force
10 100 N

Tidal current and
water resistance
6350 N

(a) Calculate the overall force acting on the *Matthew*.

Answer: .... N

(b) What effect will this have on the motion of the ship? Why?

....

....

Topic Review

Did you sail through the questions without any trouble?
Are you sure you understand all of the learning objectives?

Moments

Learning Objectives

Moments — they're all to do with forces making an object turn, and despite the confusing name, they're actually pretty simple. By the end of these pages you'll...

- know that a moment is the turning effect created by a force
- be able to calculate whether moments are balanced or unbalanced.

Forces Cause Objects to Turn Around Pivots

A pivot is the point around which rotation happens — like the middle of a see-saw.

A Moment is the Turning Effect of a Force

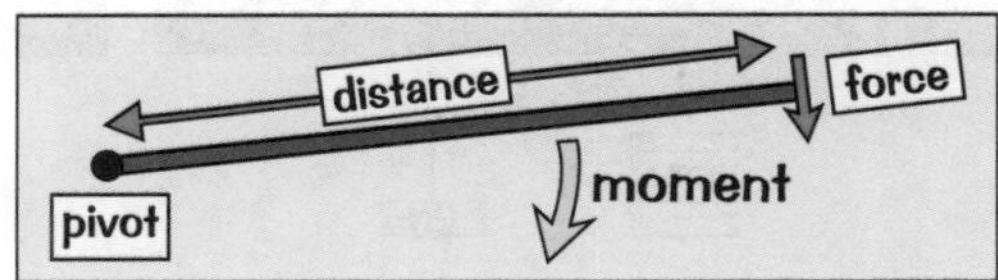

1) When a force acts on something which has a pivot, it creates a moment — a turning effect.
2) Moments are usually measured in newton metres (Nm).
3) This is the all-important formula for finding moments:

Moment = force × distance ...or **M = F × d**

(Moment in newton metres, Nm; force in newtons, N; distance in metres, m)

4) Moments can make things turn clockwise or anticlockwise.

5) If two or more moments act on a stationary object, it will stay still if the moments are balanced, or turn if they are unbalanced:

Moments Can Be Balanced...

Balanced moments mean that:

anticlockwise moments = clockwise moments

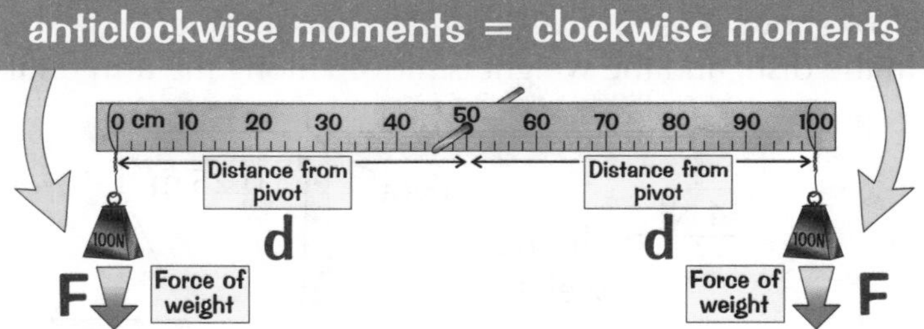

ANTICLOCKWISE			CLOCKWISE
force x distance	=	force x distance	
100 N x 0.5 m	=	100 N x 0.5 m	
50 Nm	=	50 Nm	

...or Unbalanced

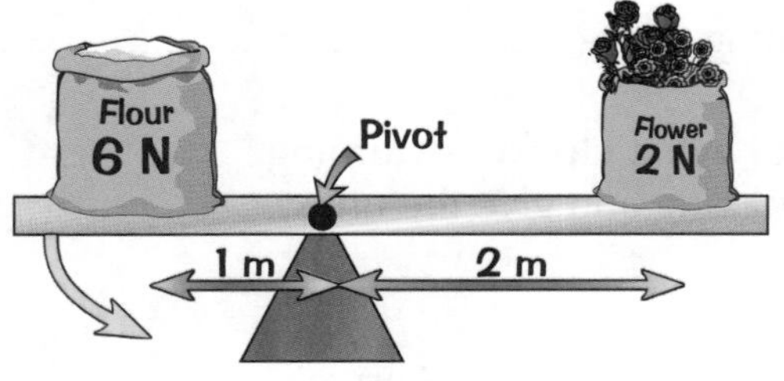

If the moments are not balanced, the object will turn in the direction of the bigger moment.

ANTICLOCKWISE: $6\ N \times 1\ m = 6\ Nm$

CLOCKWISE: $2\ N \times 2\ m = 4\ Nm$

The anticlockwise moment is bigger than the clockwise moment. The beam is NOT BALANCED.

It will TURN in the ANTICLOCKWISE DIRECTION.

Is it Balanced?

Which rulers are balanced? If you think the ruler is balanced, write balanced above it. If you reckon it's unbalanced, then write unbalanced, but say which side of the ruler will dip down too. Words to use: balanced, unbalanced, left side down, right side down. Answers on page 53.

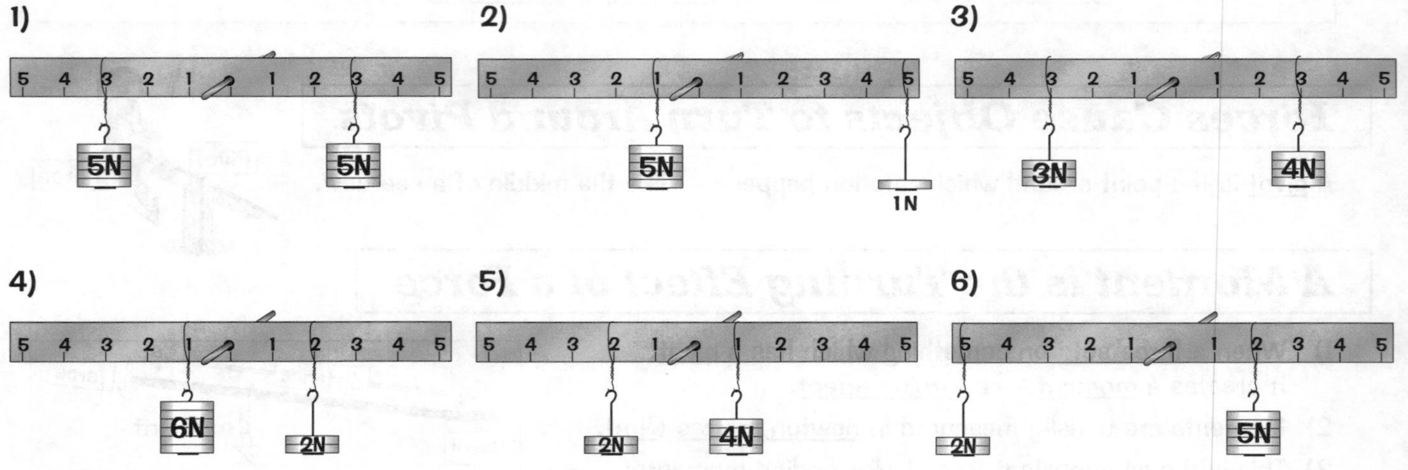

Majestically Monstrous Moments Questions

Quick Fire Questions

Q1 What is a pivot?

Q2 What is the equation for calculating moments?

Q3 If the moments are balanced, what can you say about the size of the anticlockwise and clockwise moments?

Practice Questions

Q1 The diagram below shows a set of scales used to measure rice.
Rice is placed in the dish, and the weight is moved along the arm until the scales balance.

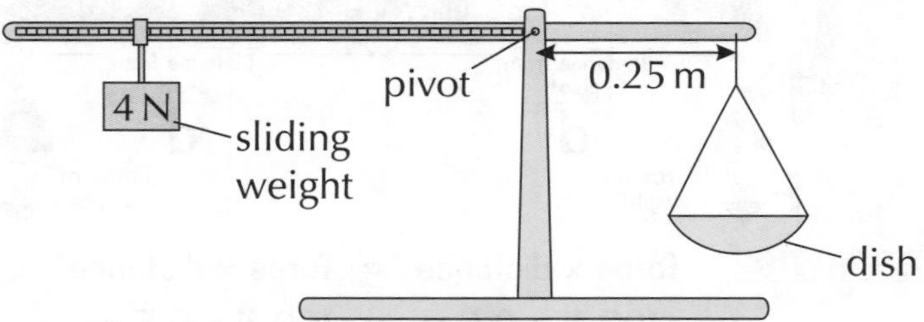

(a) The weight of the rice and of the sliding weight create turning forces about the pivot.

(i) What name is given to a turning force about a pivot?

....

(ii) What are the units used to measure such a turning force? ....

(b) A bag of rice with weight 10 N is placed in the dish. What clockwise turning force will this cause about the pivot? Show your working and give the units.

Answer: ....

(c) What distance from the pivot should the sliding weight be placed to balance the scales?

Answer: .... m

(d) What weight of rice will balance the scales if the sliding weight is 10 cm from the pivot?

Answer: .... N

Q2 Jade and her friend Ava sit on opposite sides of a see-saw.
Jade weighs 500 N and Ava weighs 400 N.

For each of these situations, find the moments caused by Jade and Ava.
Say whether the see-saw would balance, tip on Jade's side or tip on Ava's side.

(a) Jade sits 2 m from the pivot. Ava sits 1 m from the pivot.

Jade's moment: .... Nm

Ava's moment: .... Nm

The see-saw would ....

(b) Jade sits 1 m from the pivot. Ava sits 1.25 m from the pivot.

Jade's moment: .... Nm

Ava's moment: .... Nm

The see-saw would ....

Q3 (a) Jason's arm muscles exert a force at 2 cm from the elbow. The largest force that they can exert is 4000 N. What moment will this give about the elbow, in newton metres?

Answer: .... Nm

(b) Jason's hand is 40 cm away from his elbow. Will the maximum weight that Jason can hold steady in his hand be smaller or larger than 4000 N? Explain your answer.

....

....

....

Topic Review
How did you get on with the questions?
Do you feel like you could ace a surprise test on this topic?

Answers to questions on page 52: a) balanced b) balanced c) unbalanced, right side down d) unbalanced, left side down e) balanced f) balanced

Forces and Elasticity

Learning Objectives

Forces can stretch or squash objects, as well as all that other stuff. Once you've read these pages, you'll be cooler than a street-dancing bat and know that...

- forces can make objects deform (change shape) by stretching or squashing them
- work is done when an object is deformed
- Hooke's Law says the extension of a spring is directly proportional to the force
- when a weight is held still by a spring with balanced forces, it's said to be in equilibrium.

You Can Deform Objects by Stretching or Squashing

1) You can use forces to stretch or compress (squash) objects, e.g. crushing an empty can.
2) The force you apply causes the object to deform (change its shape).
3) Springs are special because they usually spring back into their original shape after the force has been removed — they are elastic.

Work is Done When a Force Deforms an Object

1) You might remember energy transfer from page 10 (if not, take a look). Work done is the same thing.
2) Energy is transferred and work is done when an object is deformed. For example:

- When you stretch or compress a spring, you're doing work.
- This transfers energy to the elastic energy store of the spring.
- When the spring 'springs' back into its original shape, the energy in the elastic energy store is transferred to it's kinetic energy store.

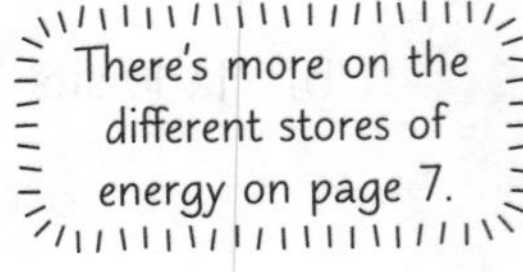

There's more on the different stores of energy on page 7.

Hooke's Law Says Extension of a Spring Depends on the Force

1) If an ordinary metal spring is supported at the top and then a weight is attached to the bottom, it stretches.
2) Hooke's Law says the amount that a spring stretches (the extension, e) is directly proportional to the force applied, F.
3) This means that the relationship between force and extension is linear.
4) k is the spring constant. Its value depends on the material that you're stretching and it's measured in newtons per metre (N/m).

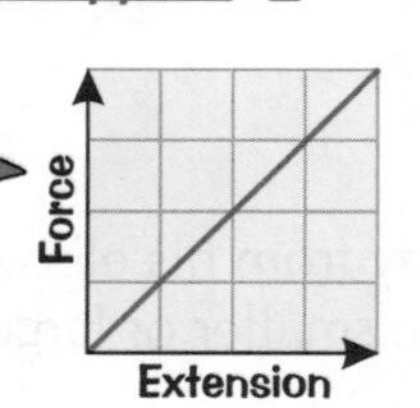

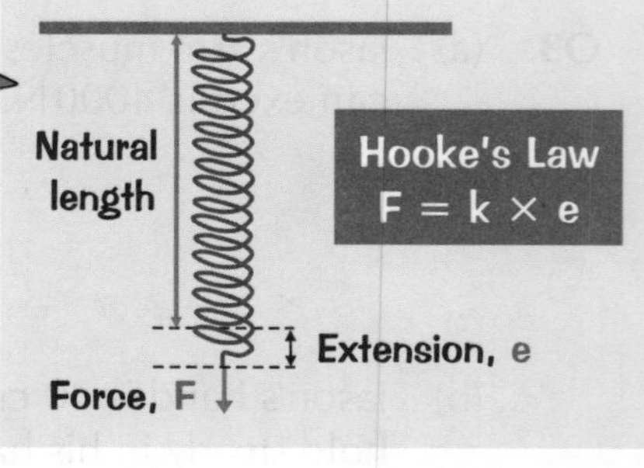

Most stretchy objects will obey Hooke's Law, but only up to a certain force — after that an object gets stretched so much that it can't 'spring back' to its original shape. Springs are unusual because the extension at which Hooke's Law stops working is much higher for them than it is for most materials.

When a Stretched Spring Holds a Weight, it's in Equilibrium

1) When a stretched or compressed spring holds a weight still, the force of the weight is the same as the force of the spring trying to return to its original shape — it's in equilibrium.
2) Equilibrium is just a fancy way of saying the forces are balanced.

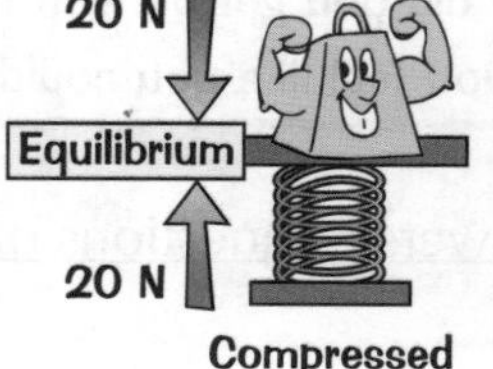

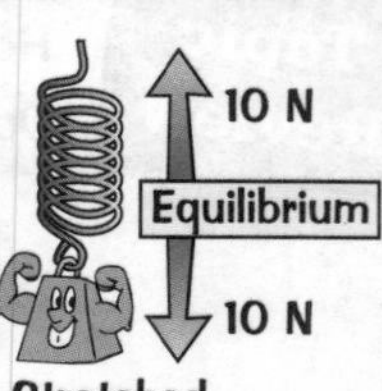

Eerily Enchanting Elasticity Questions

Quick Fire Questions

Q1 Lots of objects can be deformed. What's special about springs?

Q2 Describe what Hooke's Law says.

Q3 What does it mean to say that a compressed spring is holding a weight in equilibrium?

Practice Questions

Q1 A student is hanging blocks of different weights from a spring and measuring the extension of the spring. Her table of results is shown below. It is incomplete.

	Extension (cm)			
Weight (N)	**Reading One**	**Reading Two**	**Reading Three**	**Mean**
0.1	0.5	0.4	0.6	0.5
0.3	1.5	1.5	1.5	
0.5	2.3	2.7	2.5	
0.7	3.5	4.7	3.5	
0.9	4.2	4.6	4.7	

(a) (i) One of the student's readings was affected by a random error. Find this value in the table and put a cross through it.

(ii) Complete the final column of the table. (Ignore the value that you have crossed out — do not use it to calculate the mean.)

(b) What is the independent variable in this experiment?

....

(c) Plot a graph using the data in the table. Put weight on the horizontal axis and extension on the vertical axis. Plot the points and draw a line of best fit.

(d) Use your graph to predict the extension of the spring for a weight of 0.4 N. .... cm

Topic Review

How did you get on with the questions?
Are you confident on all the learning objectives?

Pressure

Learning Objectives

Pressure is all to do with the amount of force that's pressing on a certain area. By the time you've pressed on through these pages, you'll know...

- that pressure is force divided by area
- why air pressure decreases with height
- how pressure in liquids like water increases with depth
- about upthrust in liquids and why it can cause objects to float.

Pressure is How Much Force is Put on a Certain Area

Pressure, force and area are tied up with each other, as the formula shows.

$$\text{Pressure} = \frac{\text{Force}}{\text{Area}}$$

You can put it in a formula triangle too:

See page 36 for more on how to use formula triangles.

A given force acting over a big area means a small pressure (and vice versa).

Snow shoes (large area)
Pointy high heels (small area)
Weight is spread over a large area, so the pressure is low and he doesn't sink into the snow.
Weight is concentrated over a small area, so the pressure is high and she sinks into the snow.

Pressure is Measured in N/m² or Pascals (Pa)

If a force of 1 newton is spread over an area of 1 m² (like this) then it exerts a pressure of 1 pascal. Simple as that.

1 newton/metre² = 1 pascal
1 N/m² = 1 Pa

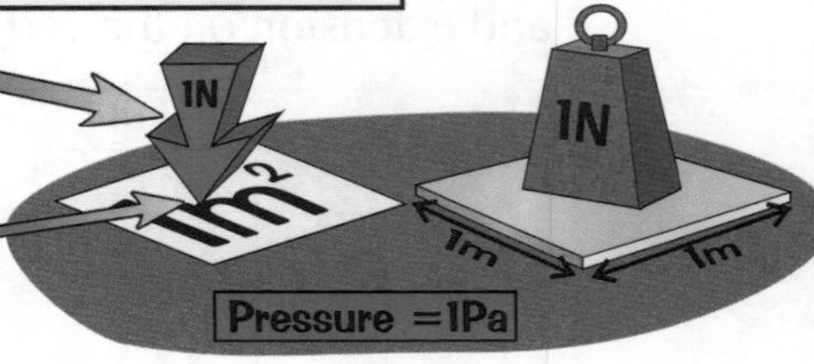

Force acts normal (at 90°) to area.

Atmospheric Pressure is All Around Us All the Time

The weight of the atmosphere is constantly pushing against us — but we're so used to it we can't feel it.

1) The lower you are, the more atmosphere there is above you — so the pressure due to the weight of the atmosphere increases.
2) If you gain height, there's less atmosphere above you, so the atmospheric pressure decreases.
3) Atmospheric pressure is over 100 000 Pa at sea level. But at the top of Mount Everest (8800 m above sea level) the atmospheric pressure is only around 33 000 Pa.

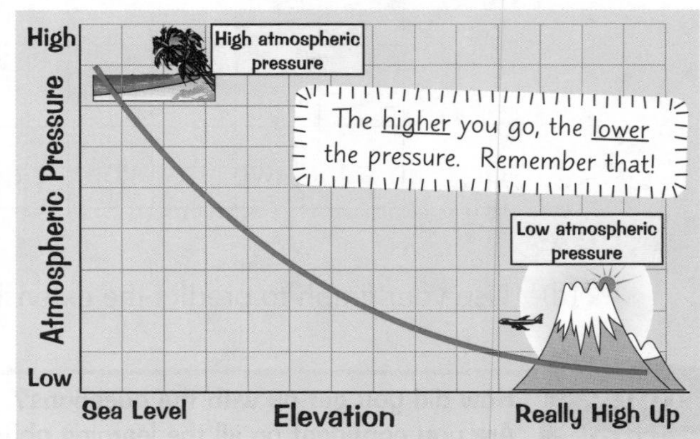

The higher you go, the lower the pressure. Remember that!

The Pressure in Liquids Increases with Depth

For liquids like water, the pressure increases with depth due to the weight of water above.

Water Pressure Causes Upthrust and Makes Things Float

1) If you submerge an object in water, it experiences water pressure from all directions.
2) Because water pressure increases with depth, the force pushing upwards at the bottom of the object is greater than the force pushing down at the top of the object.
3) This causes an overall upwards force, called upthrust.
4) A boat sinks until the upthrust is equal to its weight, — at this point the boat will start to float.
5) If the upthrust is less than the object's weight, it will sink.

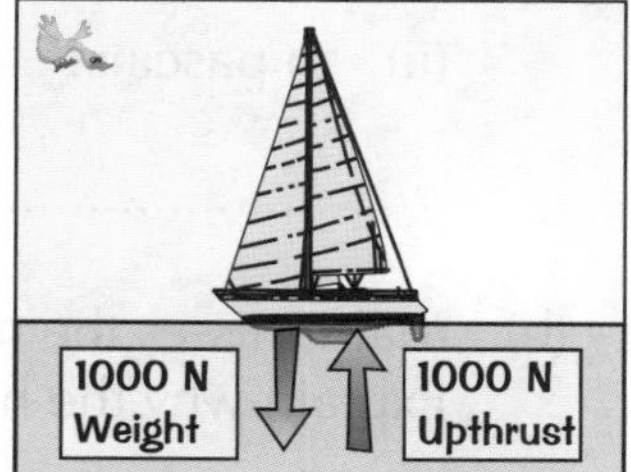

EXAMPLE: a submerged beach ball Here's a beach ball that's been pushed underwater.

- The water above the ball is pushing down on the ball with a force of 30 N.
- The weight of the ball is also pushing down on the water with a force of 1 N.
- But the water under the ball is pushing upwards with an overall force of 140 N.
- The overall force on the ball is 140 – 30 – 1 = 109 N upwards.

So the ball will rise up through the water to the surface.

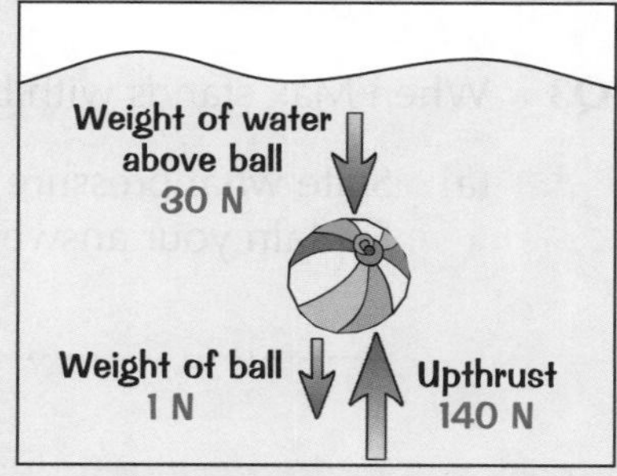

Peerlessly Practical Pressure Questions

Quick Fire Questions

Q1 Write down the formula that you would use to calculate pressure.

Q2 Give two units of pressure.

Q3 Is atmospheric pressure higher at sea level or at the top of a high mountain? Why?

Practice Questions

Q1 The diagram on the right shows a stationary personal watercraft floating in water.

The watercraft weighs 3000 N.

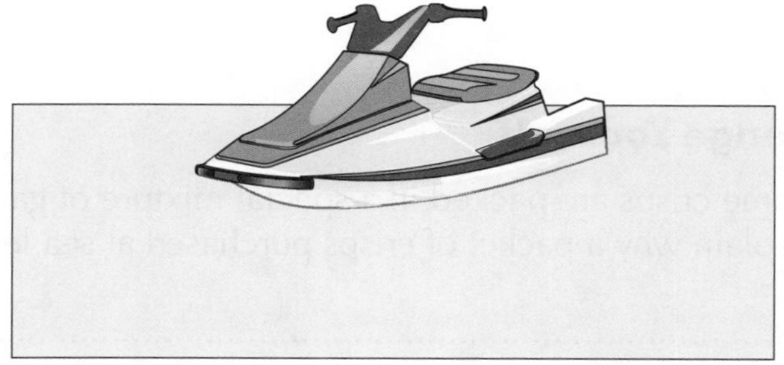

(a) Draw and label two arrows on the diagram showing the force created by the weight of the watercraft and the upthrust force from the water.

(b) Explain what stops the watercraft sinking despite its weight.

....

....

Q2 Mairi hammers a nail into a wall with a force of 12 N.

(a) The point of the nail has an area of 0.00001 m^2. What pressure is exerted by the point of the nail:

(i) in N/m^2? Show your working.

Answer: .... N/m^2

(ii) in pascals?

....

(b) Mairi misses the nail and hits the wall with the hammer.
Explain why the hammer can't penetrate the wall, even though the nail can.

....

....

Q3 When Max stands with both feet on the floor he exerts a pressure of 12 000 Pa on the floor.

(a) State what pressure Max will exert on the floor if he lifts one foot off the floor.
Explain your answer.

....

....

....

....

(b) When Max stands with both feet on the floor, the area of contact between the soles of his feet and the floor is 0.06 m^2. What does Max weigh in newtons? Show your working.

Answer: .... N

Challenge Yourself

Q4 Some crisps are packed in a special mixture of gases to ensure they remain fresh and crispy.
Explain why a packet of crisps purchased at sea level expands when taken up a very high mountain.

....

....

....

Topic Review

Did you feel confident answering the questions?
Are you sure you've got all the learning objectives sussed?

Water Waves

Learning Objectives

Water waves are exactly what they sound like — waves on the surface of water, like the ones you see at the beach. By the end of this topic, you should...

- know that water waves are an example of transverse waves
- know that transverse waves have undulations at right angles to their direction of travel
- know that water waves are reflected when they hit a surface
- understand that superposition is when two water waves meet and add or cancel.

Water Waves are Transverse

1) Waves travelling across the ocean are good examples of transverse waves.
2) A transverse wave has undulations (up and down movements) that are at right angles to the direction the wave is travelling in.

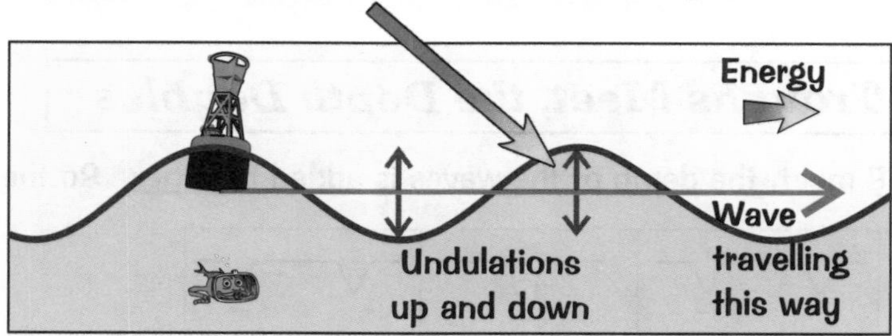

3) Waves transfer energy from one place to another. (Just think of a big wave crashing on to a beach and moving all the stones around.)
4) The undulations are also at right angles to the direction of energy transfer.
5) Lots of other important waves are transverse too, like light (see page 62).

Waves Can be Reflected

1) If a water wave hits a surface, it will be reflected.
2) This causes the direction of the wave to change.
3) All waves can be reflected. There's more on reflection on page 65.

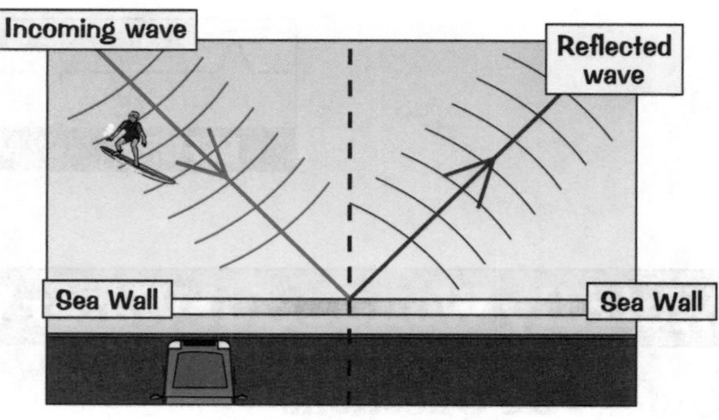

Transverse Waves Have Crests, Troughs and Displacement

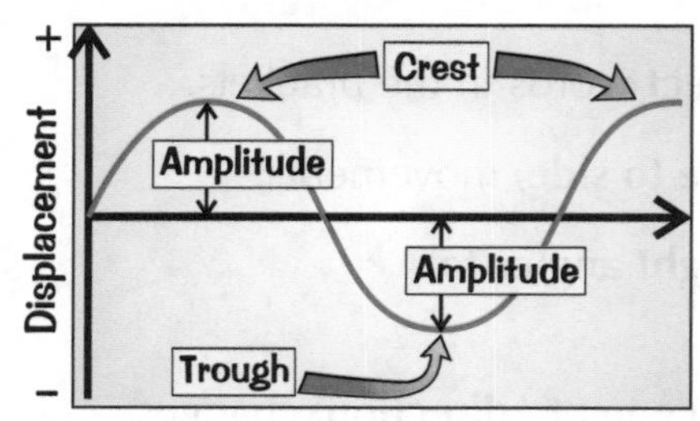

1) The crest is the highest part of the wave.
2) The trough is the lowest part of the wave.
3) The displacement is how far a point on the wave is from the middle line.
4) The amplitude is the maximum displacement — the distance from the middle of the wave to a crest or trough.

Superposition Happens When Two Waves Meet

1) If two water waves meet, their displacements will combine briefly.
2) That means that they become one single wave, with a displacement that's equal to the displacement of each individual wave added together. (See below for some nice examples.)
3) This is called superposition.
4) After combining, the waves then carry on as they were before.
5) If two waves of the same size meet during a crest or trough, one of three things will happen:

If Two Identical Crests Meet, the Height Doubles

If two identical CRESTS meet, the height of the waves is added together. So the crest height doubles.

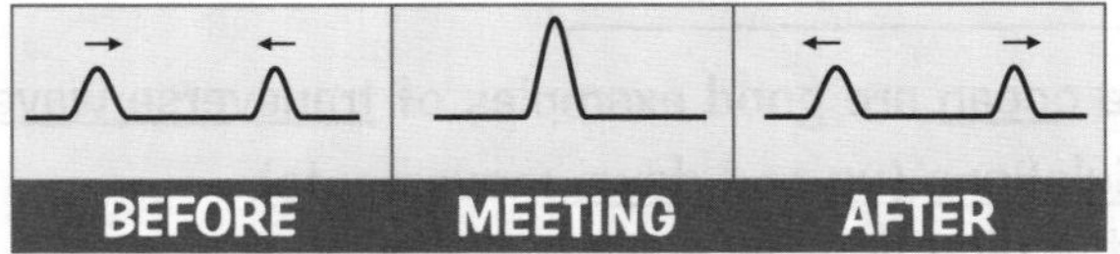

If Two Identical Troughs Meet, the Depth Doubles

If two identical TROUGHS meet, the depth of the waves is added together. So the trough depth doubles.

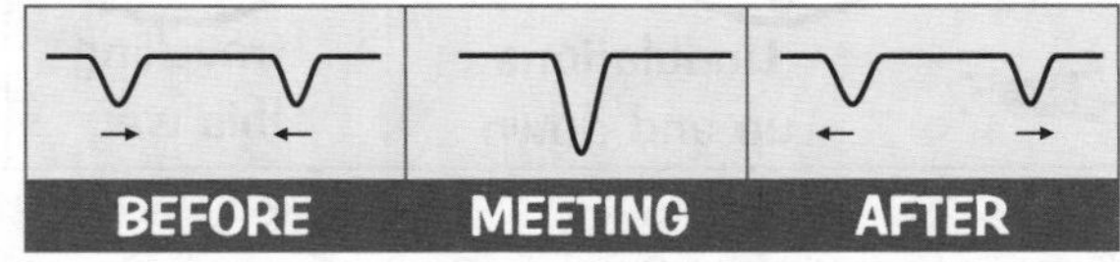

If a Crest Meets a Trough of the Same Size, They Cancel

If one wave is at a crest and the other at a trough, you subtract the trough depth from the crest height. So if the crest height is the same as the trough depth they'll cancel out, leaving a flat water surface.

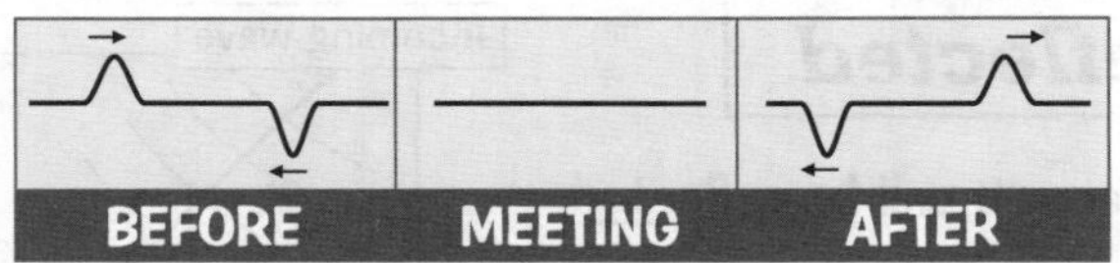

Weirdly Wonderful Water Wave Questions

Quick Fire Questions

Q1 What type of wave are water waves?

Q2 What happens when the crest of a water wave meets the crest of an identical water wave?

Practice Questions

Q1 Complete each sentence below by crossing out the **incorrect** words in the brackets.

(a) Water waves have undulations, or (**up and down / side to side**) movements.

(b) These undulations are (**in the same direction as / at right angles to**) the direction of energy transfer.

(c) Reflection is when a wave hits a surface and its (**displacement / direction**) changes.

Q2 Use words from the box to fill in the labels on the diagram of a water wave below.

Direction of energy transfer	Trough	Crest	Direction of undulations

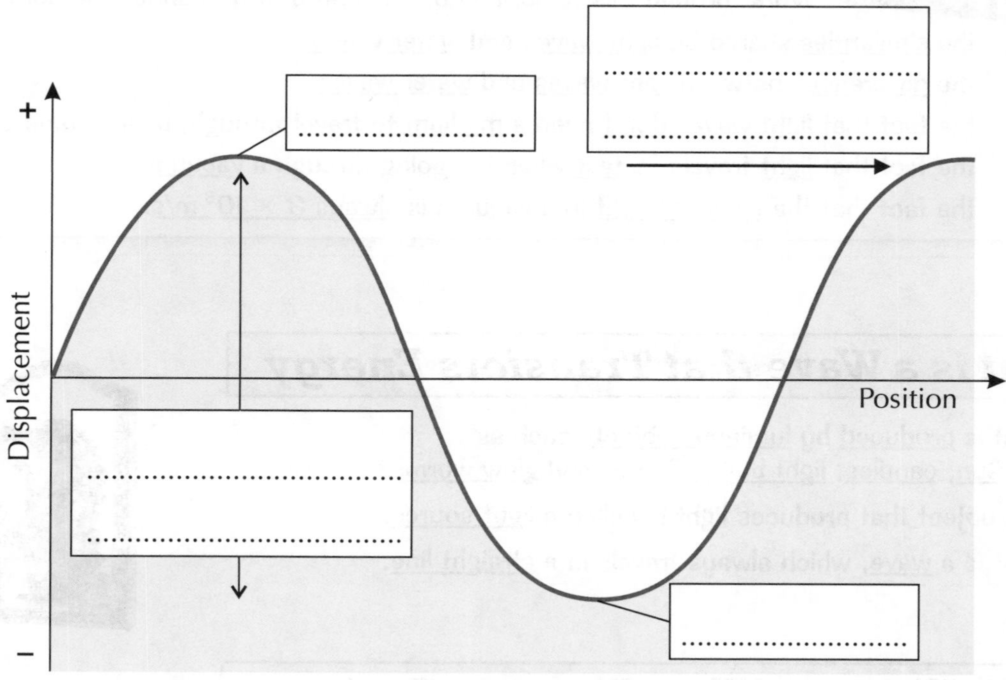

Challenge Yourself

Q3 When two water waves meet, their displacements combine briefly.

(a) What name is given to this phenomenon? ....

(b) In what situation would two waves cancel each other out completely?

....

(c) On the blank axes, sketch the wave that results from the two waves shown meeting.

(i)

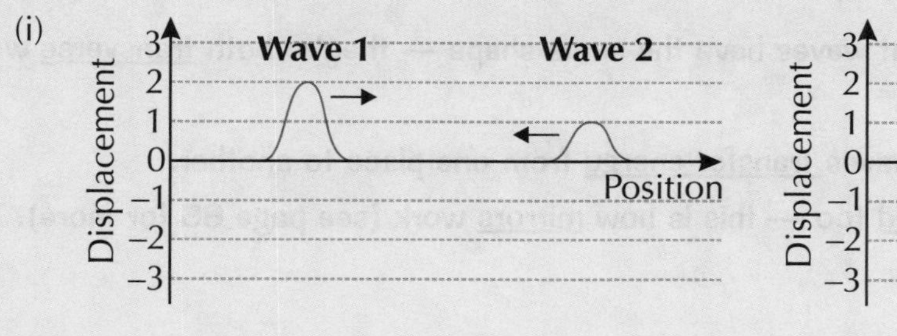

(ii)

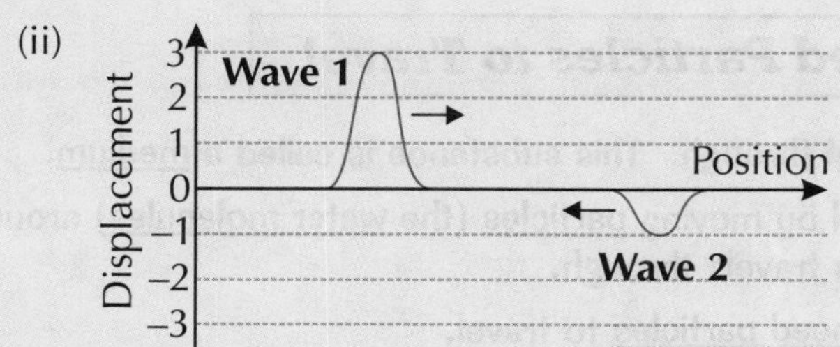

Topic Review

How did you get on with the questions?
Are you confident on all the learning objectives?

Light Waves

Learning Objectives

It might not be obvious just from looking at it, but light is actually a wave. Work through this topic, and by the end of it you should be confident with...

- the similarities shared by light waves and water waves
- the differences between light waves and water waves
- the fact that light waves don't need a medium to travel through, unlike some other waves
- the fact that light travels fastest when it's going through a vacuum
- the fact that the speed of light in a vacuum is always 3×10^8 m/s.

Light is a Wave that Transfers Energy

1) Light is produced by luminous objects such as the Sun, candles, light bulbs, flames and glow worms.
2) Any object that produces light is called a light source.
3) Light is a wave, which always travels in a straight line.

Light Waves and Water Waves Are Similar...

1) Like waves in water, light waves are transverse waves — they have undulations at right angles to the direction the wave is travelling in (see page 59).

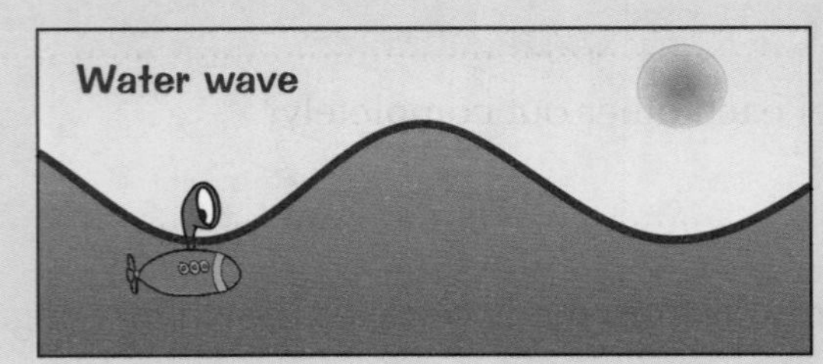

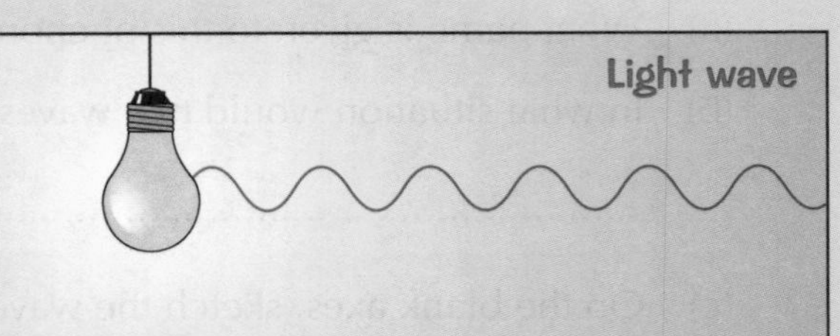

Water waves and light waves have the same shape — they're both transverse waves.

2) Like waves in water, light waves transfer energy from one place to another.
3) Light waves can be reflected too — this is how mirrors work (see page 65 for more).

...But Light Waves Don't Need Particles to Travel

1) Some waves need a substance to travel through. This substance is called a medium.
2) Water waves are like this — they travel by moving particles (the water molecules) around. Water is the medium that a water wave travels through.
3) Unlike water waves, light waves don't need particles to travel.
4) This is a good thing for us — light from the Sun has to travel through space (where there aren't many particles, see next page) to reach Earth.
5) In fact, light waves are slowed down by particles.

Light Waves Always Travel at the Same Speed in a Vacuum

1) Light travels faster when there aren't many particles to get in the way.
2) Light always travels fastest in a vacuum. A vacuum is where there is nothing at all — no air, no particles, nothing. Space is mostly a vacuum.
3) The speed of light in a vacuum is 3×10^8 m/s. (That's three hundred million metres per second.)
4) This means light from the Sun gets to Earth in just 8.3 minutes — even though it's 150,000,000 km away.

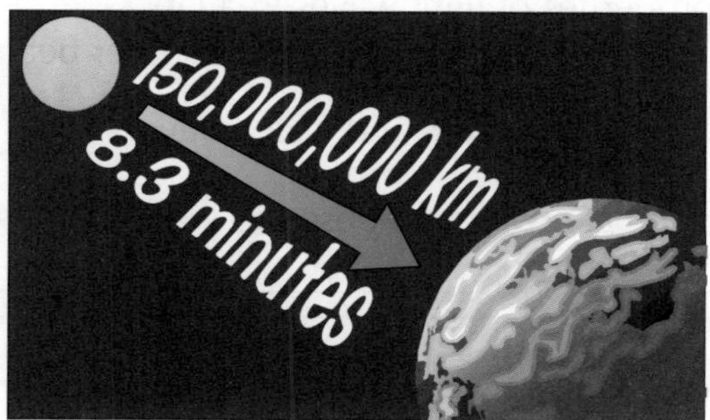

5) The speed of light in a vacuum is a constant. That means it's always the same, no matter what colour the light is.
6) Nothing travels faster than light in a vacuum.
7) Make sure that you really know this before you move on:

Speed of light waves in a vacuum= 3×10^8 m/s

8) Light will travel slower than this when it has to go through a medium (like air or water).
9) But it's still so fast that its movement appears instant to the human eye — you won't notice a delay between you pushing a light switch and the bulb lighting up at the opposite end of the room.

Lavishly Lovely Light Questions

Quick Fire Questions

Q1 Sketch a light wave coming out from a torch.

Q2 Explain why light can reach us from the Sun even though space is mostly a vacuum.

Q3 What's the speed of light in a vacuum, in m/s?

Practice Questions

Q1 Use words from the box to complete the sentences below (you don't need to use all the words).

a constant	a vacuum
a medium	variable

Light travels fastest when it's travelling through ....

In this case, the speed of light is ....

When light travels through .... it slows down.

Q2 Light travels very quickly but it still takes time to travel. Draw a line between each box on the left to the box on the right that shows roughly how long it takes light to make that journey.

across a room	eight minutes
from the Sun to Earth	almost instantly
from a distant star to Earth	many years

Q3 Jacques is investigating the properties of light waves in a lab. He uses a laser, which produces thin beams of light called laser beams.

(a) What type of wave are both light waves and water waves? ....

(b) Jacques points a laser beam at a wall and observes what happens.

Wall

Laser

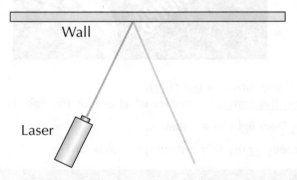

(i) Explain why the laser beam changes direction when it hits the wall.

....

Challenge Yourself

(ii) Jacques notices that the wall starts to heat up after the laser has been left on for a while. Suggest why this is, even though nothing is touching it.

....

(iii) Next, Jacques tries to measure the speed of the laser light. He fires the beam at a sensor 5 metres away that measures time to the nearest hundredth of a second. He writes down how long it took the light to reach the sensor and uses this to calculate its speed.

Suggest why he would not be able to get an accurate result using this sensor.

....

....

....

....

Topic Review

How did you find the questions?
Are you happy with all the learning objectives?

Reflection and Refraction

Learning Objectives

You've already seen that light can be reflected. Another crafty trick it has up its sleeve is refraction. Work through the topic, and by the end you should...

- know that a clear reflection off smooth surfaces, such as mirrors, is called specular reflection
- be able to use a diagram to show how mirrors reflect light
- know that rough surfaces reflect light in all different directions — this is called diffuse scattering
- know that light can pass through transparent materials, but not opaque ones
- know that when light travels from one transparent material to another, it refracts (bends).

Mirrors Have *Shiny Surfaces* Which *Reflect Light*

1) A light wave is also known as a light ray. Light rays reflect off mirrors and most other things.
2) Mirrors have a very smooth shiny surface, which reflects all the light off at the same angle, giving a clear reflection. This is called specular reflection.
3) Rough surfaces look dull, because the light is reflected back (scattered) in lots of different directions. This is called diffuse reflection (or diffuse scattering).

Smooth, shiny surface.
SPECULAR reflection.

Shiny side of mirror

Mirror

Light rays reflected off at the same angle

Rough, dull surface.
DIFFUSE scattering.

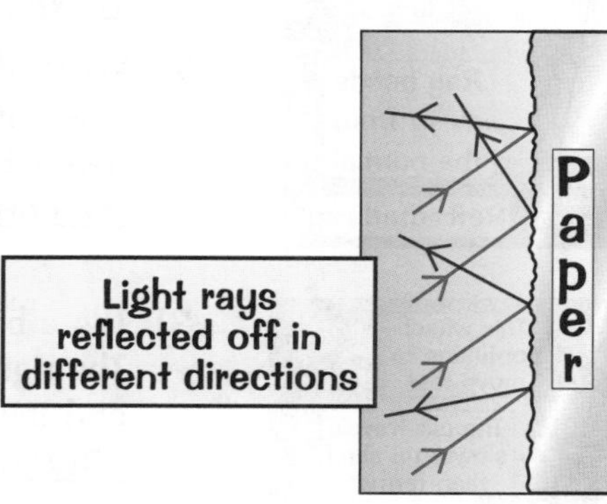

Learn the Law of Reflection:

ANGLE OF INCIDENCE = ANGLE OF REFLECTION
ANGLE i = ANGLE r

1) The normal is a line at a right angle (90°) to a mirror.
2) The incident light ray is the one travelling towards the mirror. The angle it makes with the normal is the angle of incidence, i.
3) The reflected light ray is the one travelling away from the mirror. The angle it makes with the normal is the angle of reflection, r.
4) The law of reflection says that angle i will always be the same as angle r.
5) This just means that when a ray of light hits a mirror, it will bounce off again at the same angle.

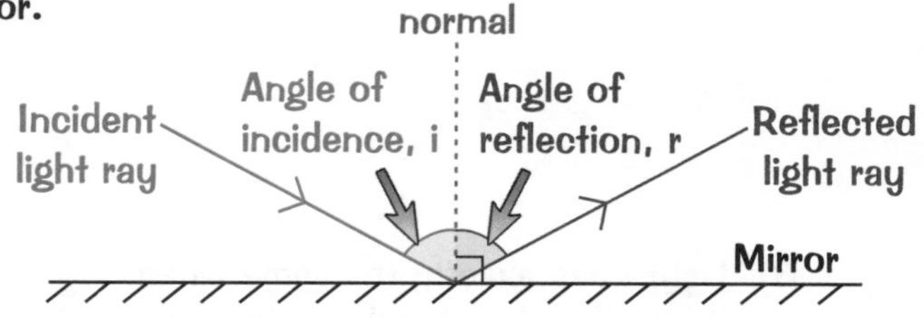

This is a ray diagram. Make sure you draw straight lines and draw the angles accurately when drawing ray diagrams (use a ruler and a protractor). Remember to put the arrows on the light rays too.

Refraction is When Light Bends as it Crosses a Boundary

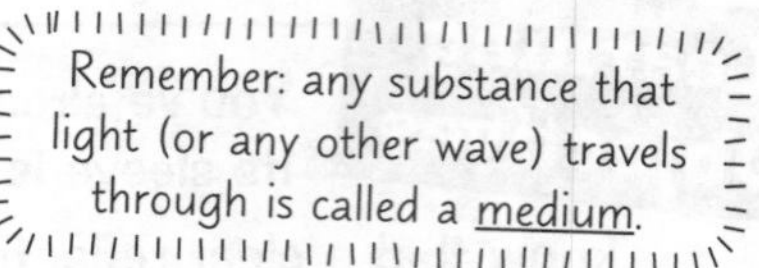

Remember: any substance that light (or any other wave) travels through is called a medium.

1) Light will travel through transparent (see-through) material, but it won't go through anything opaque (not see-through).
2) When light travels from one transparent medium to another, it bends. This is called refraction.

LEARN THESE:

When light goes from a LESS dense medium to a MORE dense medium: light bends TOWARDS THE NORMAL. — Example: air to glass.

The plural of medium is 'media'.

When light goes from a MORE dense medium to a LESS dense medium: light bends AWAY FROM THE NORMAL. — Example: glass to air.

3) This happens because light travels at different speeds through different materials (see page 63).
4) The bigger the difference in density between the materials, the more light will bend.

Light Hitting a Glass Block is Like a Car Hitting Sand

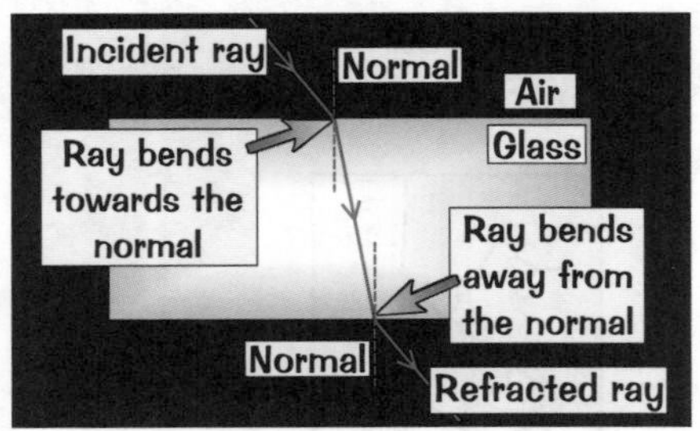

1) Light hits the glass at an angle, slows down. This makes it bend TOWARDS the normal.
2) When the light ray leaves the glass, it speeds up again and bends back AWAY from the normal.

This wheel continues to move fast
This wheel slows first
The car travels slower on sand than tarmac
Car's direction changes
This wheel speeds up
Car's direction changes

3) It's a bit like a car hitting sand at an angle. The right wheels get slowed down first and this turns the car to the right — TOWARDS the normal.
4) Leaving the sand, the right wheel speeds up first and this turns the car to the left — AWAY from the normal.
5) If both wheels hit the sand together they slow down together, so the car goes straight through, WITHOUT TURNING.

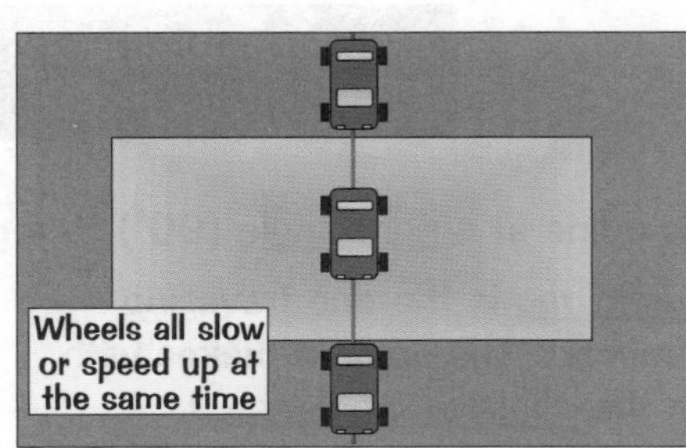

6) Light does exactly the same when it hits the glass block straight on.

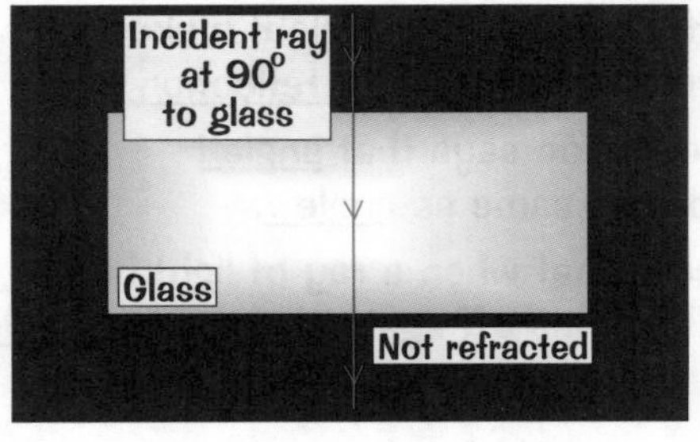

Rightfully Riveting Reflection and Refraction Questions

Quick Fire Questions

Q1 What type of reflection happens when light reflects off a shiny, smooth surface, like a mirror?

Q2 What's diffuse scattering?

Q3 Which way does light bend when it travels from air to glass?

Q4 In what situation would light **not** bend when it travels from air to glass?

Practice Questions

Q1 The diagram below shows a ray of light hitting a mirror.

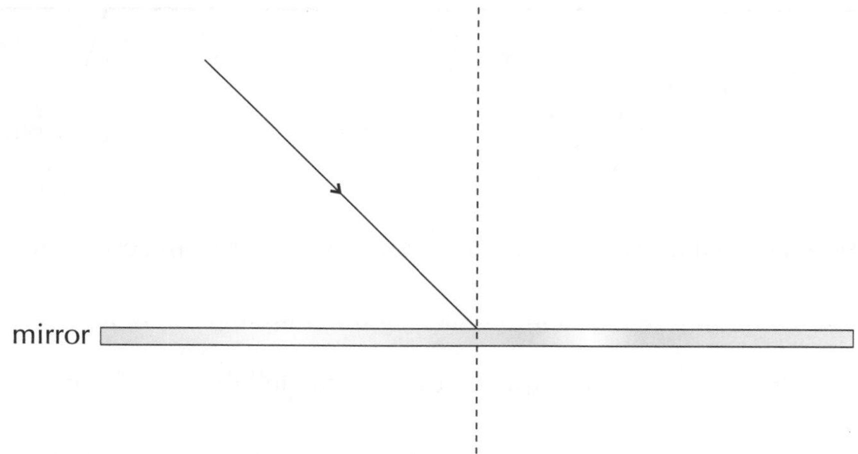

(a) Label the diagram with the correct **names** for the following.

(i) The ray of light travelling towards the mirror. (ii) The dotted line.

(b) On the diagram, draw and label

(i) The angle of incidence, i.

(ii) The reflected light ray.

(iii) The angle of reflection, r.

(c) The diagram above is an example of the law of reflection.

(i) State the law of reflection.

....

(ii) What property of the mirror means that all the light falling on it obeys the law of reflection?

....

(iii) Describe a situation where the light falling on an object does not obey the law of reflection.

....

....

Q2 Lesley is investigating how much light bends when it passes from one medium to another. She sets up two experiments. In the first one, she shines a ray of light so that it travels from air into water. In the second one, the ray travels from air into glass.

(a) Name **one** thing that Lesley should keep the same in both experiments so that she can compare the results. (WS)

....

The diagram below shows Lesley's results.

incident ray — normal — air / water — refracted ray

incident ray — normal — air / glass — refracted ray

(b) Water is more dense than air. Explain how you can tell this from Lesley's results.

....

(c) Glass is more dense than water. Explain how you can tell this from Lesley's results.

....

....

....

Challenge Yourself

(d) Complete the diagram below to show how you would expect light to bend as it travels from **water** to **glass**.

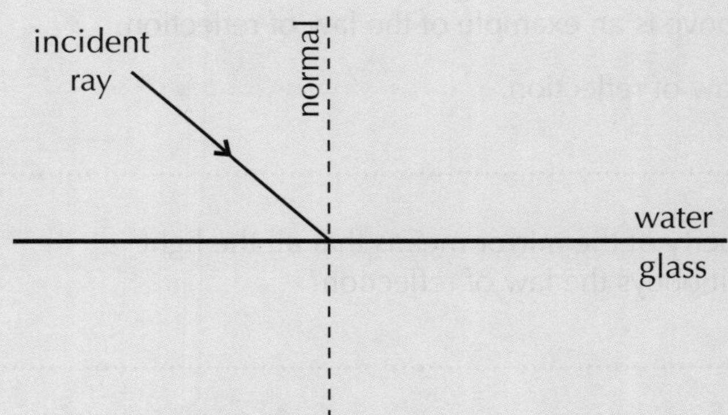

Topic Review How did you get on with the questions? Have you nailed the learning objectives?

How We See

Learning Objectives

You probably take seeing for granted without paying too much attention to it. Just remember, without light you'd be scuppered. By the end of this topic, you'll...

- know that we see non-luminous objects when light reflects off them into our eyes
- be able to describe how a pinhole camera forms images
- know that a convex lens can be used to focus light
- know the structure of the human eye and how it forms images
- know that an eye and a camera both contain photo-sensitive (light-sensitive) material
- know that energy is transferred when light from a source hits an absorber
- know that if photo-sensitive material absorbs light, it can cause electrical or chemical changes.

We See Things Because Light Reflects into our Eyes

1) When a luminous object produces light (see page 62), it reflects off non-luminous objects, e.g. you, me, books, sheep, etc.
2) Some of the reflected light then goes into our eyes and that, my friend, is how we see.

The Pinhole Camera is a Simple Camera

1) A pinhole camera is a box with a tiny hole at one end. It doesn't have a lens or any electronics.
2) Pinhole cameras can be used to form simple images on a paper screen.

1) The light travels in a straight line from the sheep to the tracing paper screen through the pinhole. Because the hole is small, only one ray gets in from each point on the sheep.
2) The image of the sheep is upside down and crossed over. This is because the light rays cross over inside the camera:

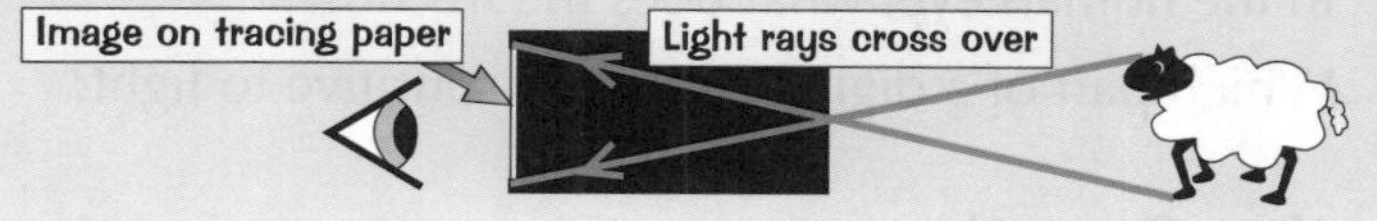

Lenses Can be Used to Focus Light

Light

Focus

Convex lens

1) A lens refracts (bends) light.
2) A convex lens bulges outwards. It causes rays of light to converge (move together) to a focus.
3) The human eye uses a combination of convex lenses to focus light — the cornea and the lens:

The CORNEA is a transparent 'window' with a convex shape. The cornea does most of the eye's focusing.

The convex LENS behind the cornea changes shape to focus light from objects at varying distances.

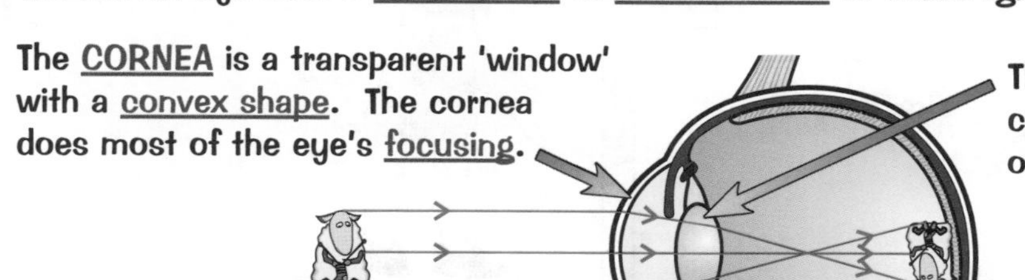

The IRIS is the coloured part of the eye. It controls the amount of light entering the eye.

Images are formed on the RETINA. Cells in the retina are photo-sensitive (sensitive to light).

Energy is Transferred From a Light *Source* to an *Absorber*

1) Energy is emitted by sources of light waves.
2) Anything that absorbs this energy is called an absorber, e.g. a retina cell in the eye, the film in a film camera or the digital image sensor in a digital camera.
3) Energy is transferred when light waves hit an absorber.

When light waves hit a retina cell, the energy it transfers causes chemical and electrical changes in special cells that send signals to the brain.

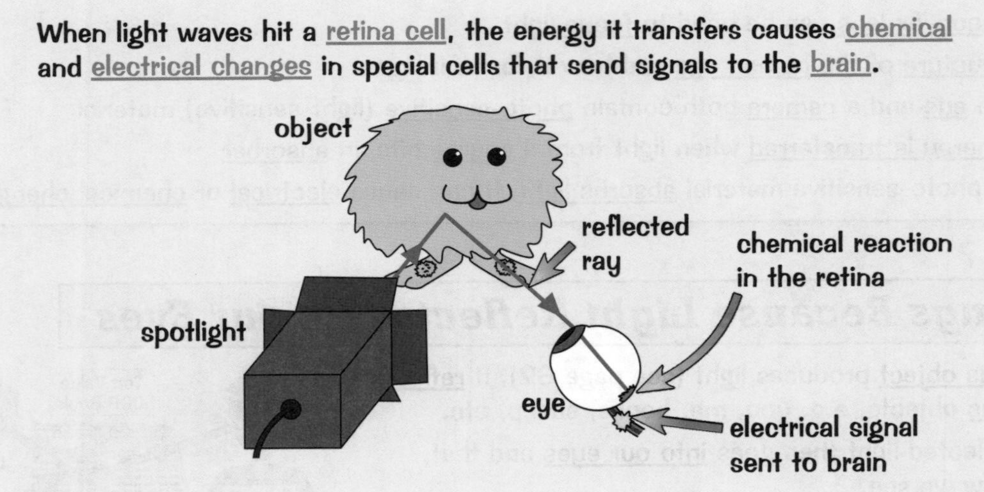

In a digital camera, light waves cause the digital image sensor to generate an electrical charge. The changes in charge are read by a computer and turned into an image.

Strangely Satisfactory Questions on How We See

Quick Fire Questions

Q1 What does a convex lens do to light?

Q2 In the human eye, what does the iris do?

Q3 Which part of a digital camera is sensitive to light?

Practice Questions

Q1 Charmaine enters a dark room, and switches on a table lamp. There is a mug on the table in front of her.

(a) Draw a ray of light on the diagram above to show how Charmaine is able to see the mug on the table.

(b) Using the diagram you completed in (a), explain how Charmaine is able to see the mug.

....

....

Q2 The pinhole camera in the diagram below is used to trace an image of a tree.

(a) Draw light rays to show how the image of the tree is formed on the tracing paper screen.

(b) Explain why the image of the tree appears upside down.

....

....

Q3 Luminous objects emit light. This light transfers energy when the light rays hit an absorber.

(a) Which part of the eye usefully absorbs energy from luminous objects?

....

(b) What happens when this part of the eye absorbs the energy?

....

....

(c) Before the eye can usefully absorb energy, the light must be focused.

(i) Which **two** parts of the eye focus light from objects?

....

(ii) Complete the diagram below by drawing two rays of light, one from the top of the object and one from the bottom, showing how they are focused by the eye to form an image.

Topic Review Did you feel confident answering the questions? Are you sure you've got all the learning objectives sussed?

Colour

Learning Objectives

Ever wondered where rainbows come from? The information in this topic might just blow the shoes right off your feet. By the end of it, you should know...

- that white light is made up of all the colours of the rainbow
- that a prism can split white light up into all of its different colours — this is called dispersal
- how the frequency of light affects its colour
- that coloured filters absorb different colours of light, only letting certain ones through
- that the colour of an object depends on what colours of light it reflects.

White Light is Not just a Single Colour

1) Bit of a shocker, I know — but white light is actually a mixture of colours.
2) This shows up when white light hits a prism or a raindrop. It gets dispersed (split up) into a full rainbow of colours.
3) The proper name for this rainbow effect is a spectrum.
4) Learn the order that the colours come out in:
   Red Orange Yellow Green Blue Indigo Violet
   Remember it with this historical jollyism:
   Richard Of York Gave Battle In Velvet

The Colour of a Light Wave is Related to Its Frequency

1) The frequency of light is the number of waves that pass a point per second.
2) Light waves increase in frequency from red (low frequency) to violet (high frequency).

Coloured Filters Only Let Their Colour Through

1) A filter only allows one particular colour of light to go through it.
2) All other colours are ABSORBED by the filter — so they don't get through.

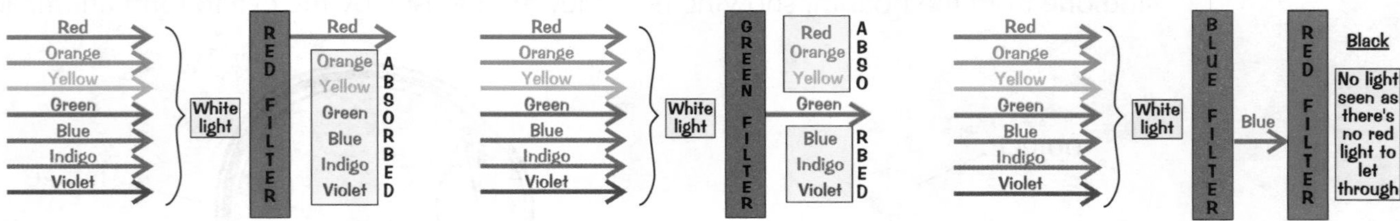

Coloured Objects Reflect Only That Colour

1) Blue jeans are blue because they diffusely reflect blue light and absorb all the other colours.
2) White objects REFLECT all colours.
3) Black objects ABSORB all colours.

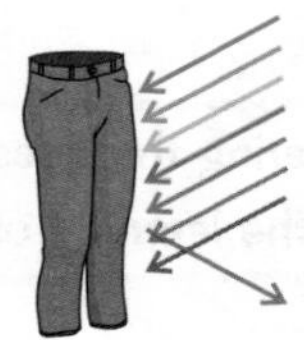

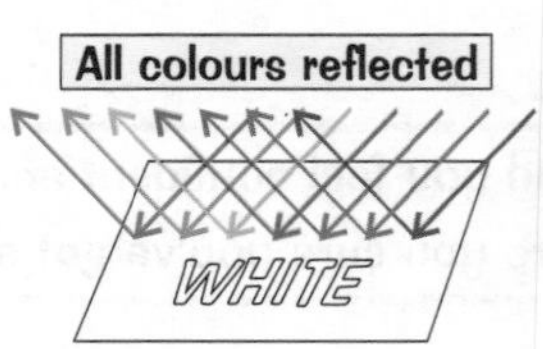

Objects Seem to Change Colour in Coloured Light

What colour an object looks in coloured light depends on which colours of light it can reflect. For example:

1) The boot looks red — it reflects red light and absorbs all other colours.
2) The lace looks green — it reflects green light and absorbs all other colours.

1) The boot looks red — it reflects the red light.
2) The lace looks black — it has no green light to reflect and it absorbs all the red light.

1) The boot looks black — it has no red light to reflect and it absorbs the green light.
2) The lace looks green — it reflects the green light.

Cautiously Cool Colour Questions

Quick Fire Questions

Q1 List the colours of the rainbow, in order.

Q2 Why can't red light pass through a green filter?

Q3 What colour would blue jeans appear in green light?

Practice Questions

Q1 When white light shines on a glass prism it bends and is split up into different colours. A rainbow pattern appears on the screen.

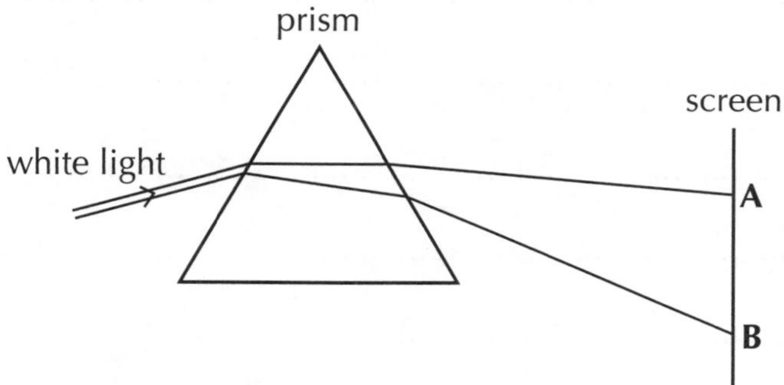

(a) What term is used to describe

(i) The rainbow pattern on the screen? ....

(ii) The splitting of light into different colours? ....

(b) (i) Name the colour that appears at **A** on the screen. ....

(ii) Name the colour that appears at **B** on the screen. ....

(c) Complete each sentence below by crossing out the **incorrect** word in the brackets.

(i) The white light entering the prism contains (**none** / **all**) of the colours of the rainbow.

(ii) The light is split because each colour has a different (**frequency** / **speed**).

(iii) The colour of light with the lowest frequency is (**red** / **violet**).

Challenge Yourself

Q2 Eric sets up the four experiments shown below to investigate how colours of light and filters can change the way objects look.

He uses a poppy from his garden. In daylight it has a red flower and green leaves.

He also uses a magenta filter, which absorbs all colours of light except red and blue, and a blue filter, which absorbs all colours of light except blue.

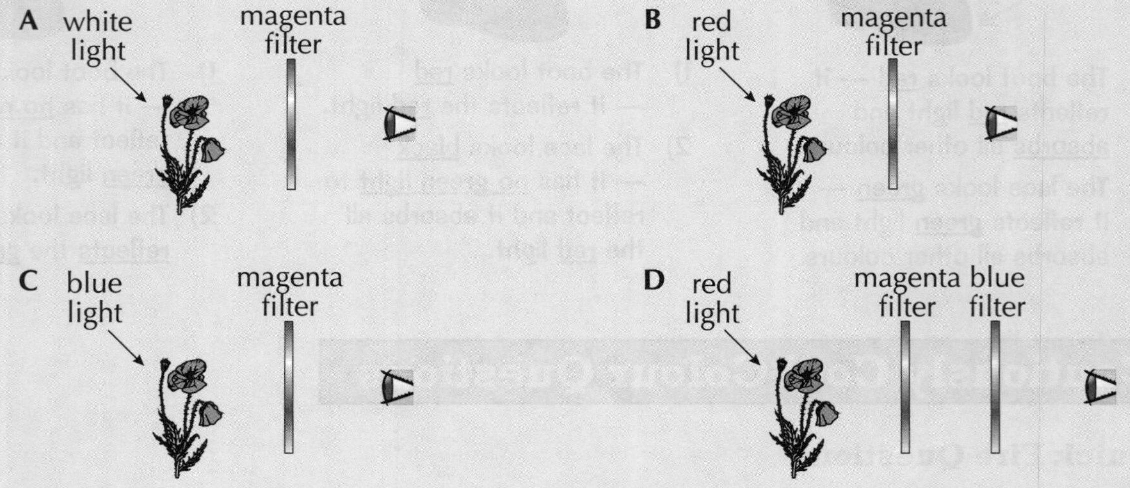

(a) For each experiment, state what colour the poppy **flower** will appear to be when Eric looks at it through the filter, and explain your answer.

A: ....

....

B: ....

....

C: ....

....

D: ....

....

(b) What colour will the poppy's **leaves** appear in all the experiments? Explain your answer.

....

....

....

Topic Review Did you sail through the questions without any trouble? Are you sure you understand all of the learning objectives?  

Sound

Learning Objectives

Sound is a wave just like light, though they do have their fair share of differences. Give these pages a read through and by the end of the topic you'll hopefully...

- know what longitudinal waves are
- know that sound waves are longitudinal waves
- know that sound waves need a medium to travel
- understand that sound can be reflected and absorbed, and know what causes echoes
- appreciate the difference in the speed of sound in air, water and solids
- understand how frequency affects the pitch of sound.

Longitudinal Waves Have Vibrations Along the Same Line

1) Longitudinal waves have vibrations that are parallel to the direction of the wave.
2) This is the kind of wave you get when you push a slinky spring back and forth:

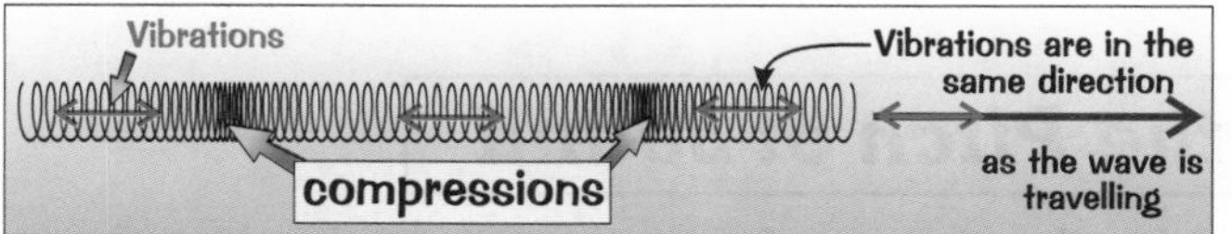

Compressions are just regions of squashed-up particles.

3) The vibrations of a longitudinal wave are also parallel to the direction of energy transfer.
4) Sound waves are another example of longitudinal waves.

Sound Travels as a Longitudinal Pressure Wave

1) Sound waves are caused by vibrating objects.
2) Sound needs a medium (e.g. air or water) to travel through because something has to pass on the vibrations — neighbouring particles need to bump into each other for the wave to travel.
3) The vibrations are passed through the medium as a series of compressions.

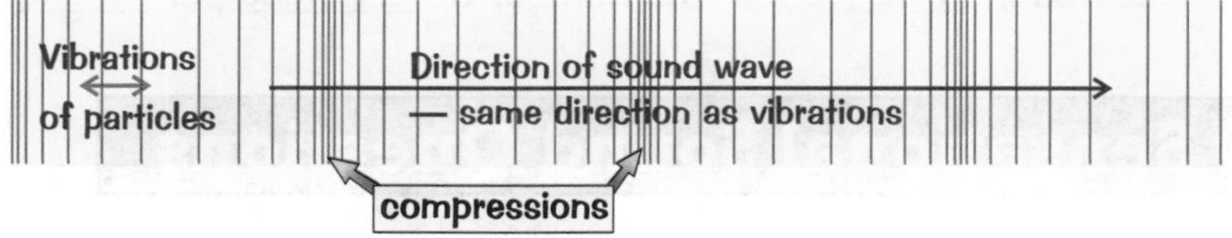

4) Sound can't travel in space, because it's mostly a vacuum (there are no particles).

Sound Can be Reflected and Absorbed

1) Sound can be reflected and refracted just like light (see page 65).
2) An echo is sound being reflected from a surface.

3) Sound can also be absorbed. Soft things like carpets, curtains, sheep, etc. absorb sound easily.

The Speed of Sound Depends On What it's Passing Through

1) The more particles there are in a given space, the faster a sound wave travels.
2) Dense media have lots of particles in a small space. So the denser the medium, the faster sound travels through it — it's easier to pass vibrations on when the particles are packed together tightly.
3) This means that sound generally travels faster in solids (like wood) than in liquids (like water) — and faster in liquids than in gases (like air).

Solid — particles are densely packed, waves travel quickly.

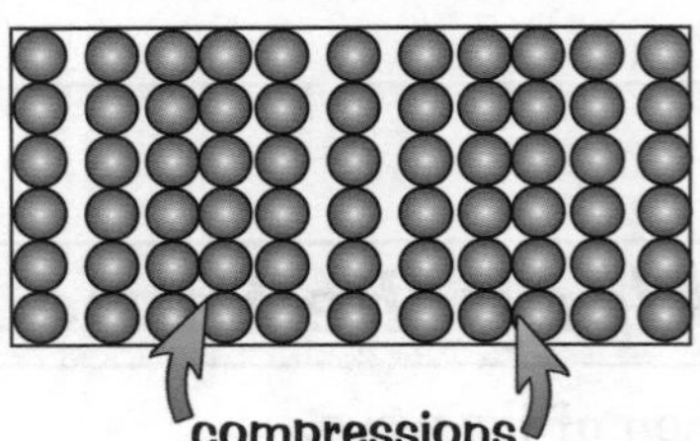

Water — particles are fairly close together, waves travel at a reasonable speed.

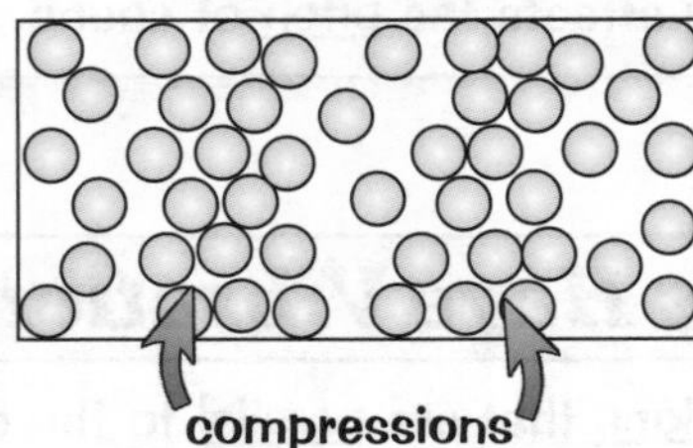

Air — particles are pretty far apart, waves travel slowly.

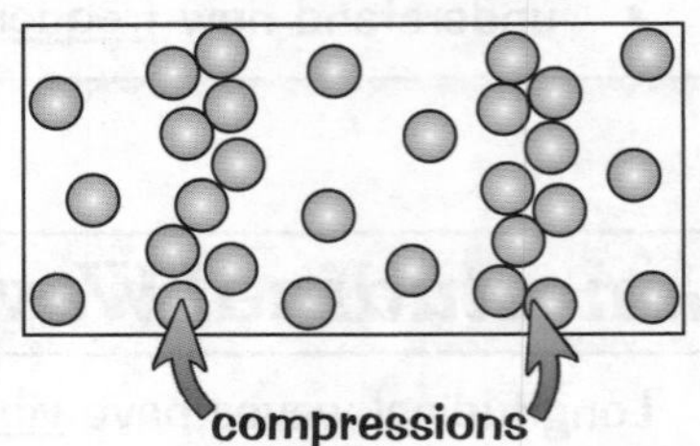

4) Sound travels much slower than light.

Frequency is the Pitch of Sound

1) The frequency of sound is the number of complete waves that pass a point per second. A high frequency means more vibrations per second.
2) Frequency is a measure of how high-pitched (squeaky) the sound is. A high frequency means a high-pitched sound.

Mosquitos make a high-pitched sound — there are lots of vibrations in a small amount of time.

Toads make a low-pitched sound — vibrations are few and far between.

3) Frequency is measured in hertz (Hz) — the number of vibrations per second.

Sonorously Sensational Sound Questions

Quick Fire Questions

Q1 What type of wave are sound waves?

Q2 In which of these does sound travel fastest: air, water, or a solid?

Q3 What's the unit used to measure the frequency of sound?

Practice Questions

Q1 Joel and Zach are astronauts. They are working on the outside of a new space station, which means they have to work in the vacuum of space.

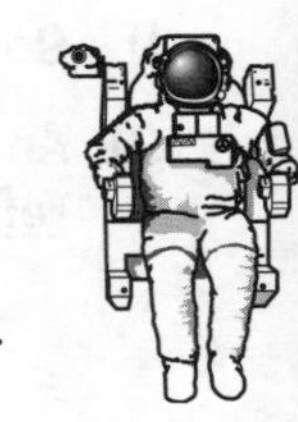

(a) Explain why Joel and Zach can see each other but must use radios to hear each other.

....

....

(b) Joel's radio fails. Describe how the sound of Zach's voice reaches Joel if they put their helmets together so that they touch.

....

....

....

Q2 Yasmin stands at the mouth of a cave and claps her hands. She hears the clap twice, first at the time she claps her hands and then again a few moments later.

(a) (i) What term is used to describe the sound when Yasmin hears it the second time?

....

(ii) What happened to the sound waves before she heard the sound the second time?

....

(b) Explain why there is a delay before Yasmin hears the sound for the second time.

....

(c) The second time Yasmin hears the sound it is fainter. Suggest why.

....

Q3 Four traces of sound waves with different frequencies are shown below.

a car engine | a scream | a dentist's drill | a road drill

(a) (i) What is meant by the **frequency** of a wave?

....

(ii) Describe the relationship between the frequency of a noise and the way it sounds.

....

(b) Write the noises shown in the diagram above in order of frequency, lowest first.

1. ....

2. ....

3. ....

4. ....

Topic Review

How did you get on with the questions?
Do you feel like you could ace a surprise test on this topic?

Hearing

Learning Objectives

Hear ye, hear ye, this topic is the most interesting yet. And if you disagree with that, I don't want to hear it. Work through this topic and you'll...

- know that sounds are made by vibrating objects
- know that sounds are detected in the human ear by the ear drum
- understand what's meant by an auditory range in humans and animals.

Sound Waves Make Your Ear Drum Vibrate

1) It's your ear drum that detects any sound that enters your ear.
2) When a sound wave hits it, the ear drum vibrates and signals are produced to send to the brain:

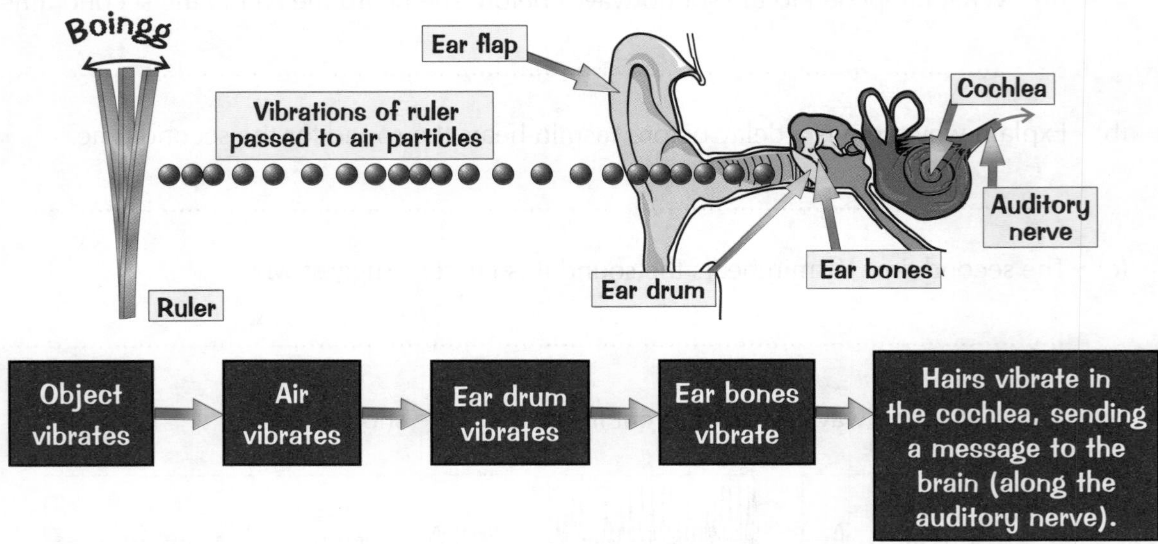

Object vibrates → Air vibrates → Ear drum vibrates → Ear bones vibrate → Hairs vibrate in the cochlea, sending a message to the brain (along the auditory nerve).

People and Animals Have Different Auditory Ranges

Your AUDITORY RANGE is the range of frequencies (vibrations per second) that you can hear.

See the previous topic for more on frequency.

1) The auditory range of humans varies a lot — but it's typically 20-20 000 Hz.
2) This means we can't hear low-pitched sounds with frequencies of less than 20 Hz or high-pitched sounds above 20 000 Hz.
3) Some animals like dogs, bats and dolphins can hear much higher frequencies than humans, as the chart shows.
4) Here are some examples of different sounds and their frequencies:

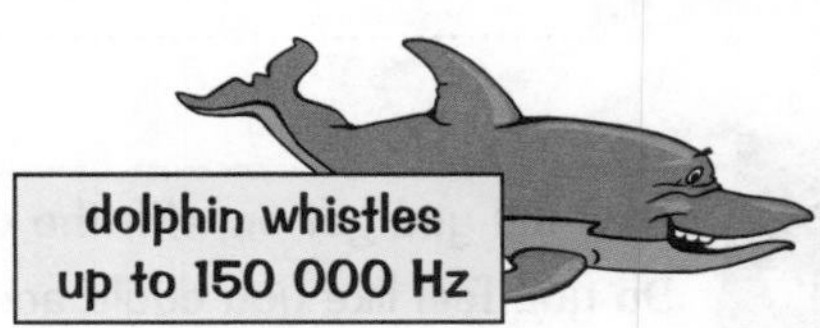

Healthily Hearty Hearing Questions

Quick Fire Questions

Q1 What does the term 'auditory range' mean?

Q2 What's the typical auditory range of a human being?

Q3 Name an animal with an auditory range greater than that of humans.

Practice Questions

Q1 Lila whispers to Heather during a lesson.

(a) Label the following parts of Heather's ear on the diagram below.

ear drum **cochlea** **ear bones** **auditory nerve**

(b) When Lila whispers, the vocal cords in her throat vibrate. Use the diagram to help you describe what happens to these vibrations so that Heather hears them as the sound of Lila's whisper.

Q2 Matthew is carrying out an experiment to find the highest frequency of sound that people in his class can hear. He sets up a speaker that can play sounds of different frequencies. Each person being tested sits with their back to the speaker and raises their hand every time they hear a sound from it. (WS)

(a) Briefly describe what Matthew could do to find the highest frequency sound a person can hear.

(b) Give **two** things that should be kept the same for each person to make it a fair test.

1.

2.

Topic Review How did you get on with the questions? Are you confident on all the learning objectives?   

Energy and Waves

Learning Objectives

The transfer of energy by sound waves can be put to good use. Read through this topic, and by the end of it you should hopefully know that...

- sound waves transfer energy, and can also be used to transfer information
- this energy and information is transferred by the vibration of particles
- sound waves are detected in microphones by vibrations of a diaphragm, and then converted to electrical signals
- loudspeakers create sound waves through vibrations of a diaphragm
- ultrasound waves can be used to clean delicate objects or treat physiotherapy patients.

Information Can be Transferred by Pressure Waves

1) All waves transfer energy from one place to another. In doing so, they can also transfer information.
2) Sound waves do this through vibrations between particles.
3) Pressure changes are caused by the particles moving side to side, which leads to some regions of the material squashing up and to others spreading out.

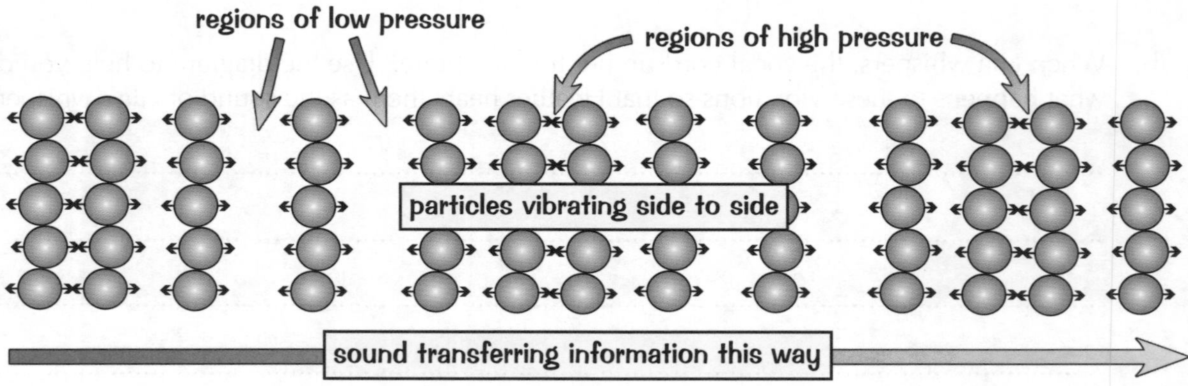

4) As the sound waves travel through a medium, it vibrates in time with the pressure changes.
5) This is very useful for recording and replaying sounds.

Sound Waves are Detected by Diaphragms in Microphones

1) The vibrations in a sound wave make a sensitive diaphragm (e.g. a thin paper or plastic sheet) vibrate inside the microphone.
2) The microphone converts the vibrations to electric signals.
3) Another device can record the electrical signals so that the sound can be reproduced later.

Loudspeakers Recreate Sound Waves

1) An electrical signal is fed into a loudspeaker.
2) This signal causes the diaphragm to vibrate.
3) This makes the air vibrate, producing sound waves It's a bit like a microphone in reverse.

Ultrasound is High Frequency Sound That We Can't Hear

1) Ultrasound includes all sounds that have a higher pitch than the normal auditory range of humans.
2) So that's any sound over 20 000 Hz.

Ultrasonic Cleaning Uses Ultrasound

High-frequency sound waves are used to clean things — energy transferred by the pressure waves dislodges dirt in tiny cracks that wouldn't normally be cleaned.

1) An item is placed in a special bath filled with water (or another liquid).
2) High-pressure ultrasound waves cause bubbles to form in cavities (holes).
3) The bubbles knock any bits of dirt (contaminants) off the object, leaving it clean enough to eat your dinner off.

You can use ultrasonic cleaning to clean jewellery, false teeth, fountain pen nibs, etc.

Ultrasound Physiotherapy May be Helpful

1) Ultrasound pressure waves transfer energy through matter — so they can reach inside your body.
2) Some physiotherapists think that this means ultrasound can be used to treat aches and pains in parts of the body that are hard to access — like muscles and tendons deep inside your shoulders.

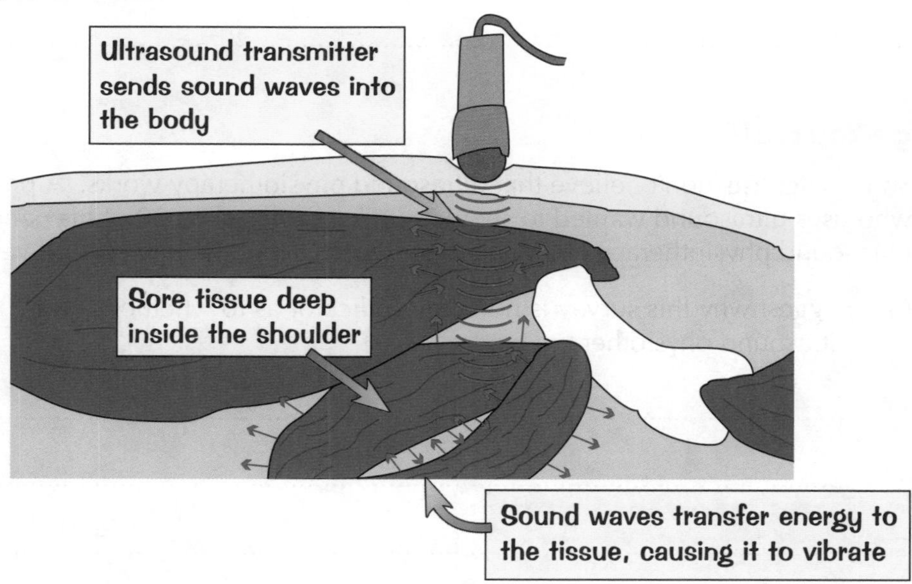
Ultrasound transmitter sends sound waves into the body
Sore tissue deep inside the shoulder
Sound waves transfer energy to the tissue, causing it to vibrate

3) But scientists have found little evidence that ultrasound physiotherapy is an effective treatment.

Endearingly Wondrous Energy and Wave Questions

Quick Fire Questions

Q1 How do sound waves transfer information?

Q2 Which part of a speaker vibrates when it creates sound waves?

Q3 What is ultrasound?

Q4 Explain how ultrasound can be used to clean false teeth.

Practice Questions

Q1 Use words from the box to complete the sentences below.

diaphragm	**electrical**	**energy**	**pressure**

Sound waves transfer .... and information through .... changes.

Microphones detect this information through vibrations in a ....

After the microphone has detected the information, it converts it to .... signals.

Q2 In ultrasound physiotherapy, the ultrasound transmitter contains a loudspeaker. The loudspeaker creates pressure waves that are sent into the patient.

(a) How does the loudspeaker produce sound waves from electrical signals?

....

....

(b) Explain why ultrasound physiotherapy may be particularly useful when the sore tissue is deep inside the body.

....

....

Challenge Yourself

(c) Some scientists don't believe that ultrasound physiotherapy works. A physiotherapist who uses ultrasound wanted to show it works, so he asked 20 of his patients whether ultrasound physiotherapy has worked for them. 16 of them answered yes.

WS (i) Suggest why this survey is not a fair indicator as to whether or not ultrasound physiotherapy works.

....

....

....

WS (ii) Another physiotherapist suggests that they should carry out a scientific study. She suggests that they should study hundreds of people rather than 20. Explain why she suggests using a larger test group.

....

....

....

Topic Review

How did you find the questions?
Are you happy with all the learning objectives?

Electrical Circuits

Learning Objectives

Read on to discover the shocking truth about electrical circuits. After these pages you'll hopefully know...

- that electric current is the flow of charge around a circuit
- that potential difference pushes current around a circuit
- that resistance slows down current and is measured in ohms (Ω)
- that resistance is given by potential difference ÷ current
- the difference between electrical conductors and insulators.

Electric Current is the Flow of Charge

1) Electric current is the flow of charge around a circuit.
2) It can only flow if a circuit is complete.
3) The moving charges are electrons — tiny particles with a negative charge.
4) Irritatingly, they flow the opposite way to the direction of conventional current, which is shown on circuits as arrows pointing always from positive to negative.

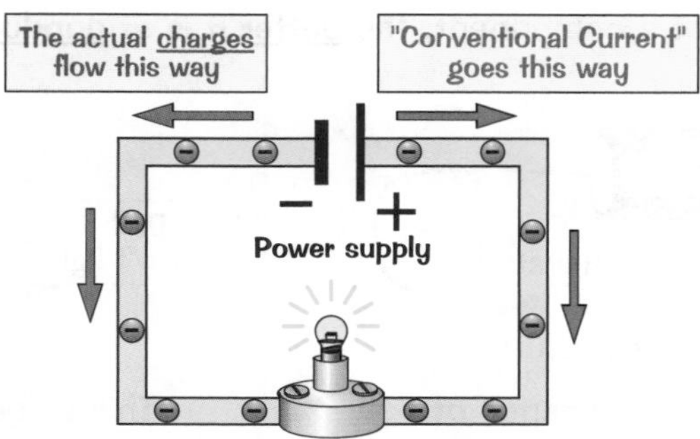

5) It's vital that you realise that CURRENT IS NOT USED UP as it flows through a circuit. The total current in the circuit is always the same.

Current is a bit like water flowing...

The pump drives the water along like a power supply. The water is there at the pump and is still there when it returns to it — and just like the water, electric current in a circuit doesn't get used up either.

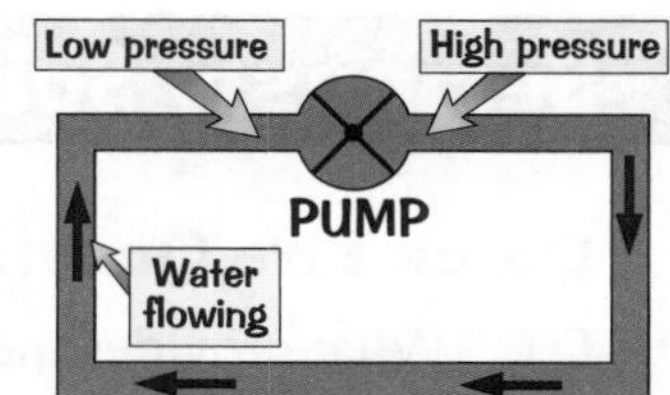

Potential Difference Pushes the Current Around

1) In a circuit the battery acts like a pump — it provides the driving force to push the charge around the circuit. This driving force is called the potential difference (or p.d.)
2) If you increase the potential difference more current will flow.
3) Different batteries have different potential differences. You can put several batteries together to make a bigger potential difference too.
4) To find the total potential difference, just add the potential difference of each battery.

Potential difference is sometimes called voltage.

Example: What is the potential difference provided by three 5 volt batteries?

Answer: The potential difference of each battery is added together.
So potential difference = 5 + 5 + 5 = 15 volts.

Resistance is *How Easily* Electricity *Can Flow*

1) Resistance is anything in a circuit that slows down the flow of current. It is measured in ohms (Ω).
2) You can calculate the resistance of a component by finding the ratio of the potential difference and current. This is just a fancy way of saying:

A component is anything you put in a circuit.

RESISTANCE = POTENTIAL DIFFERENCE ÷ CURRENT

Example: A light bulb has a current of 10 A flowing through it when a potential difference of 240 V is put across it. What is the resistance of the light bulb?

Answer: Resistance = Potential difference ÷ Current. Resistance = 240 ÷ 10 = 24 Ω.

3) This means that as long as the potential difference stays the same, the higher the resistance of a component, the smaller the current flowing through it.

Low Resistance Means a *Good Conductor*

1) Conductors are materials that allow electricity to pass through them easily — such as metals.
2) Insulators are materials that don't allow electricity to pass through them easily — such as wood.
3) The lower the resistance of a component, the better it is at conducting electricity.

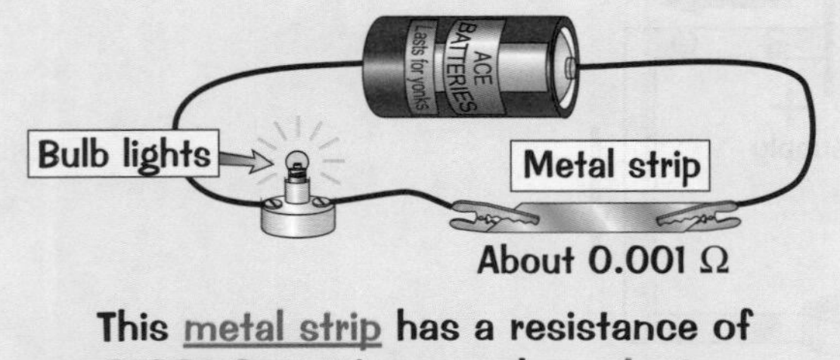

This metal strip has a resistance of 0.001 Ω — it's a good conductor.

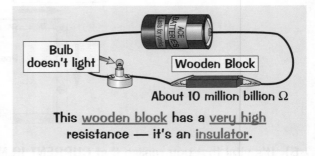

This wooden block has a very high resistance — it's an insulator.

Seriously Scintillating Circuit Questions

Quick Fire Questions

Q1 What provides the potential difference in a circuit?

Q2 Assuming the potential difference stays the same, what effect will increasing the resistance of a component have on the current flowing through it?

Q3 Which have a higher resistance, insulators or conductors?

Practice Questions

Q1 (a) What are the moving charges that make up an electric current?

....

(b) Are these charges positive or negative?

....

Q2 The diagram below shows a simple circuit, containing a power supply and a bulb.

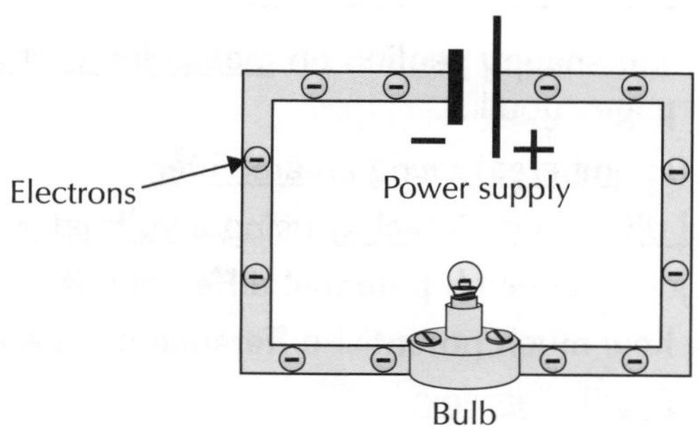

(a) Add two arrows to the diagram and label them 'direction of conventional current' and 'flow of charge'.

(b) What would happen if there was a break in the circuit?

....

(c) What would happen to the current if the potential difference of the battery was increased?

....

(d) An electric circuit can be compared to a system of water pipes. Complete the sentences below.

(i) The current is like the water because ....

....

(ii) The battery is like a pump because ....

....

Challenge Yourself

Q3 Three materials were put, one at a time, in an electrical circuit with a 2.4 V battery. The current in each material was measured and is shown in the table below.

Fill in the rest of the table by calculating the resistance of each piece of material. Use the results to say whether you think each material is a conductor or an insulator.

Material	Potential Difference (V)	Current (A)	Resistance (Ω)	Conductor or insulator?
A	2.4	0.00024		
B	2.4	16		
C	2.4	10		

Topic Review How did you get on with the questions? Do you feel like you could ace a surprise test on this topic?   

Measuring Current and Voltage

Learning Objectives

Here comes a short and snappy section on measuring current and voltage.
By the end of these pages you'll...

- know that you measure current (in amperes) using an ammeter
- know that you measure potential difference (in volts) using a voltmeter
- know that a battery rating tells you how much potential difference the battery provides
- know that a bulb rating tells you how much potential difference can be safely put across the bulb
- be able to understand and draw circuit diagrams.

Ammeters Measure Current

1) Ammeters measure electric current. It's measured in amperes (or amps, A, for short).
2) You measure the current flowing through a circuit by inserting the ammeter into the circuit like this:

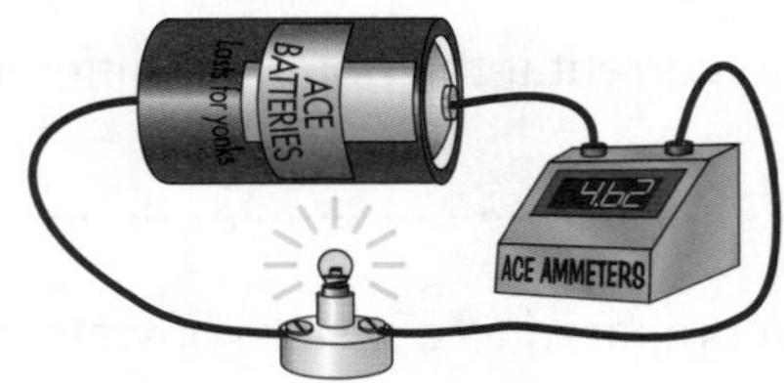

3) Remember — current doesn't get used up, so the current through the ammeter is the same as through the bulb.

Voltmeters Measure Potential Difference

1) Voltmeters measure potential difference in volts (or V for short).
2) You measure the potential difference across something in the circuit, such as a bulb.
3) To measure the potential difference across a bulb, you'd connect a voltmeter across it like this:

Batteries and Bulbs Have Potential Difference Ratings

1) A battery potential difference rating tells you the potential difference it will supply.
2) A bulb rating tells you the maximum potential difference that you can safely put across it.

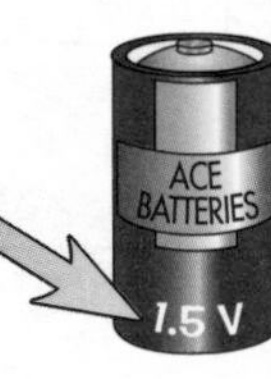

Remember, a larger potential difference means that more current flows through a circuit.
A bulb can only have so much current flowing through it before it breaks.

Circuit Diagrams Represent Real Circuits

Circuit diagrams are just simplified drawings of real circuits. You start at the cell or battery and go round the circuit, putting in a symbol for each component:

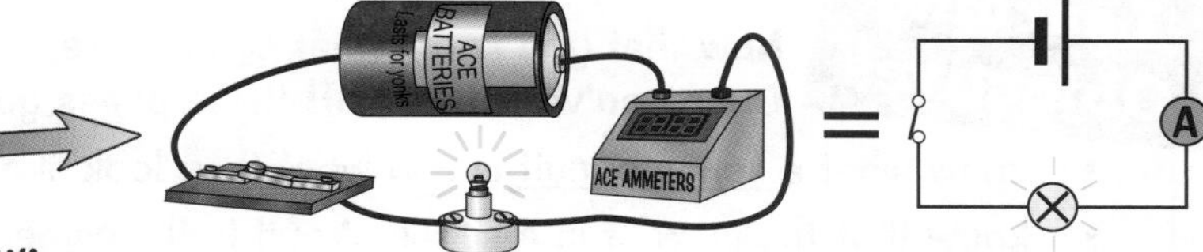

Here are the circuit symbols you need to know:

A cell = (a single source of potential difference)

A battery = (a battery is two or more cells put together)

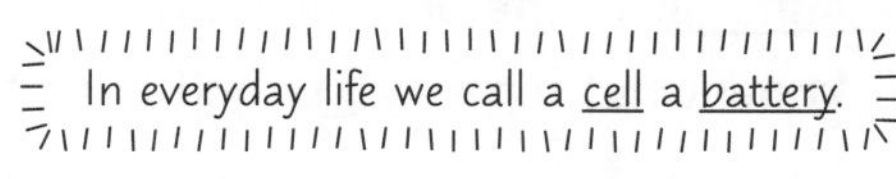

In everyday life we call a cell a battery.

A bulb =

A motor =

A voltmeter =

A switch:

A buzzer =

Curious Current and Victorious Voltage Questions

Quick Fire Questions

Q1 What does a battery rating tell you?

Q2 Why do bulbs have potential difference ratings?

Practice Questions

Q1 Complete each question below by filling in the blanks.

(a) Current is measured in .... using an ....

(b) Potential difference is measured in .... using a ....

Q2 Draw circuit diagrams for each of the circuits below.

(a)

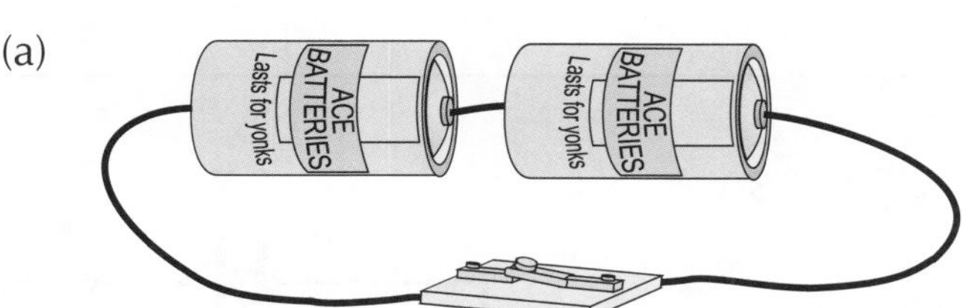

(b)

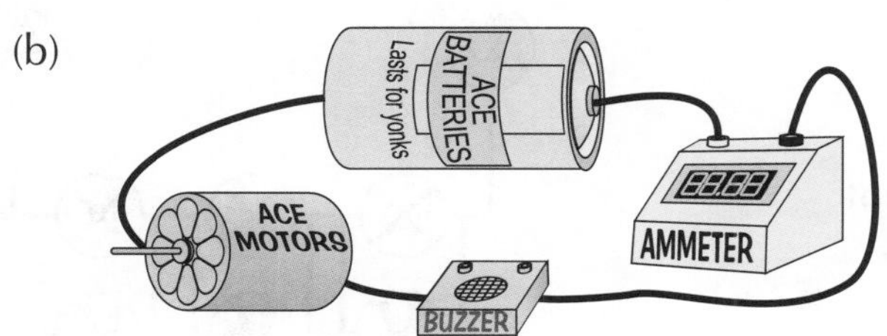

Topic Review

Did you sail through the questions without any trouble?
Are you sure you understand all of the learning objectives?

Series and Parallel Circuits

Learning Objectives

Now that you know what circuits are, it's time to find out about different kinds. Once you've finished off these pages you'll...

- know what a series circuit is and what they look like
- know that the current in a series circuit is the same in every part of the circuit
- know that the potential difference across each component in a series circuit adds up to the potential difference of the cell
- know what a parallel circuit is and what they look like
- know that the current in each branch of a parallel circuit adds up to the total current in the circuit
- know that the potential difference across each branch in a parallel circuit is the same.

Series Circuits — Current has No Choice of Route

1) In the circuit on the right current flows out of the cell, through the ammeter, the bulbs, then through the other ammeter and the switch and back to the cell. As it passes through, the current transfers energy to the bulbs.

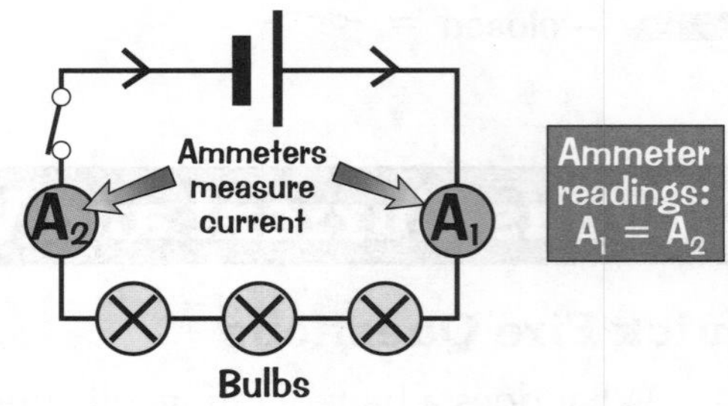

Ammeter readings: $A_1 = A_2$

2) The current is the same anywhere in this circuit as the current has no choice of route. Did I tell you current isn't used up — well don't forget.

In series circuits the current is either on or off — the switch being open or any other break in the circuit will stop the current flowing everywhere.

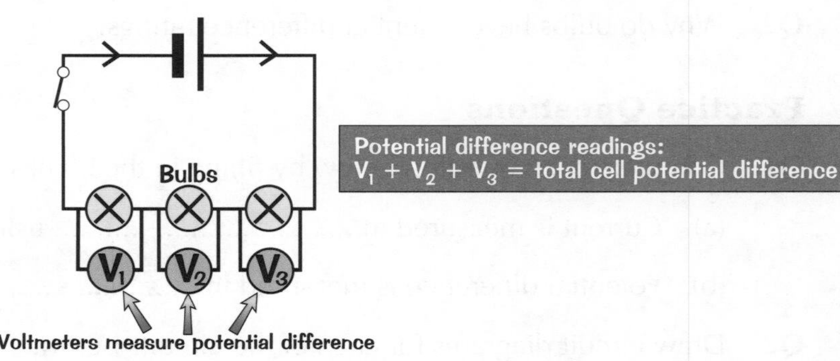

Potential difference readings: $V_1 + V_2 + V_3$ = total cell potential difference

3) In series circuits, the potential differences across the components add up to the potential difference of the cell (or battery).

EXAMPLE:

Look at the circuit shown. It has a cell with a rating of 3 V.

(a) Find the current measured at A_2.

Current is the same everywhere in the circuit.

$A_2 = A_1 = 0.3$ A

(b) Find the potential difference measured at V_2.

The potential difference across each component adds up to the potential difference of the cell.

$V_1 + V_2 + V_3 = 3$

So $V_2 = 3 - V_1 - V_3$

$= 3 - 1.5 - 0.6 = 0.9$ V

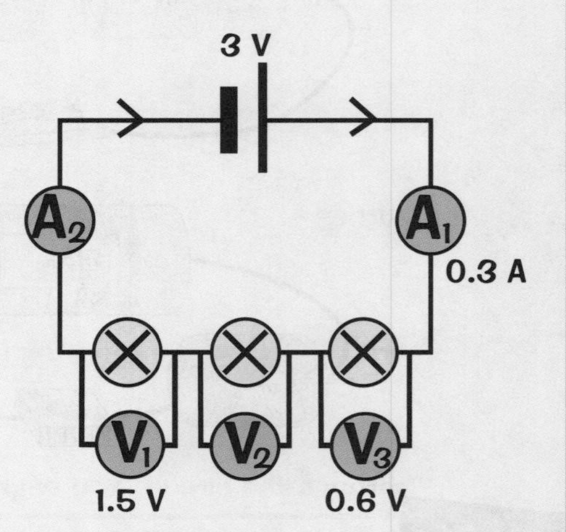

Parallel Circuits — Current has a Choice

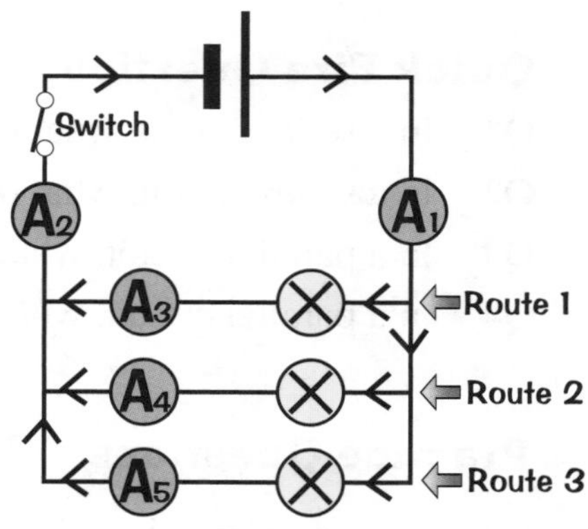

1) In the circuit shown, current flows out of the cell and it all flows through the first ammeter A_1. It then has a "choice" of three routes and the current splits down routes 1, 2 and 3.
2) The readings of ammeters A_3, A_4 and A_5 will usually be different, depending on the resistances of the components — i.e. the bulbs.
3) The three currents join up again on their way back to the cell. So the readings of $A_3+A_4+A_5$ added together will be equal to the reading for current on ammeter A_2 (which will also equal A_1).
4) It's difficult to believe I know, but the current through A_1 is the same as the current through A_2 — the current is NOT USED UP. (I may have told you that once or twice already.)
5) In parallel circuits, the potential difference across each bulb is equal to the potential difference of the cell. It doesn't matter how many branches there are — the potential difference across each is the same.

EXAMPLE:
Look at the circuit shown. It has a cell with a potential difference of 3 V.

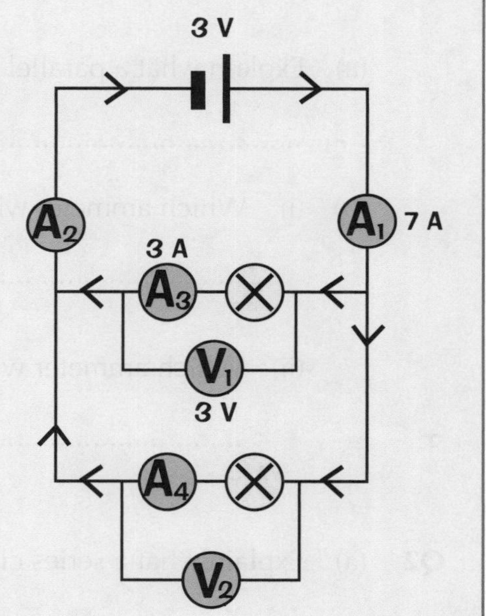

(a) Find the potential difference measured at V_2.

In a parallel circuit the potential difference across each branch is the same as the potential difference of the cell.

V_2 = potential difference of the cell = V_1 = 3 V

(b) Find the current measured at A_2.

The current which flows into the cell will be the same as the current which flows out.

$A_2 = A_1 = 7\ A$

(c) Find the current measured at A_4.

The current flowing through each branch will add up to the current through A_1 or A_2.

$A_3 + A_4 = A_1$

So $A_4 = A_1 - A_3$

$= 7 - 3 = 4\ A$

Different Parts of a Parallel Circuit can be Turned On and Off

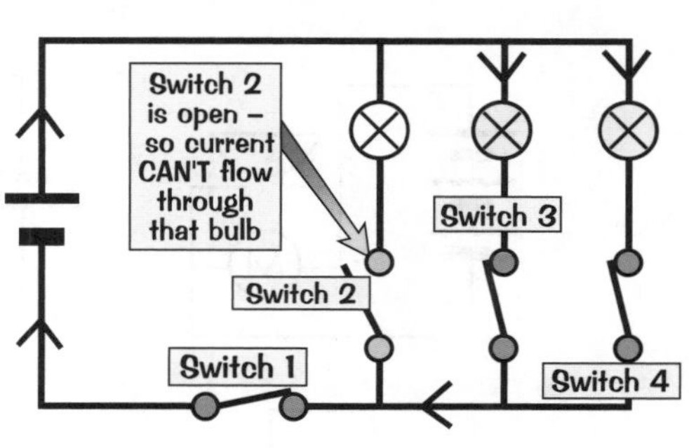

1) In the circuit on the right, the different bulbs can be turned on and off using switches 2, 3 and 4.
2) At the moment, switch 2 is open, so the bulb on that branch is off. All the other switches are closed, so the other two bulbs are on.
3) Opening switch 1 would cause all three bulbs to turn off, as there'd be no way for current to flow from the battery, through the circuit, and back to the battery.
4) As long as switch 1 is closed though, closing any of the other switches will turn on the bulb in that branch.

Splendid Series and Perfect Parallel Circuit Questions

Quick Fire Questions

Q1 In a series circuit, what do you know about the current through each component?

Q2 In a series circuit, what does the potential difference across each component add up to?

Q3 In a parallel circuit, what does the current in each branch add up to?

Q4 In a parallel circuit, what do you know about the potential difference across each branch?

Practice Questions

Q1 The diagram below shows a parallel circuit with two bulbs, a motor, and four ammeters.

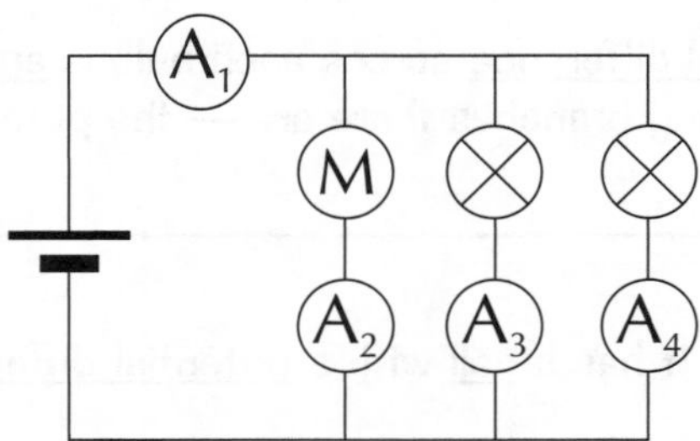

(a) Explain what a parallel circuit is.

....

(b) (i) Which ammeter will show how much current is flowing through the whole circuit?

....

(ii) Which ammeter will show how much current is flowing through the motor?

....

Q2 (a) Explain what a series circuit is.

....

....

(b) Put a tick below any of these diagrams that represent series circuits.

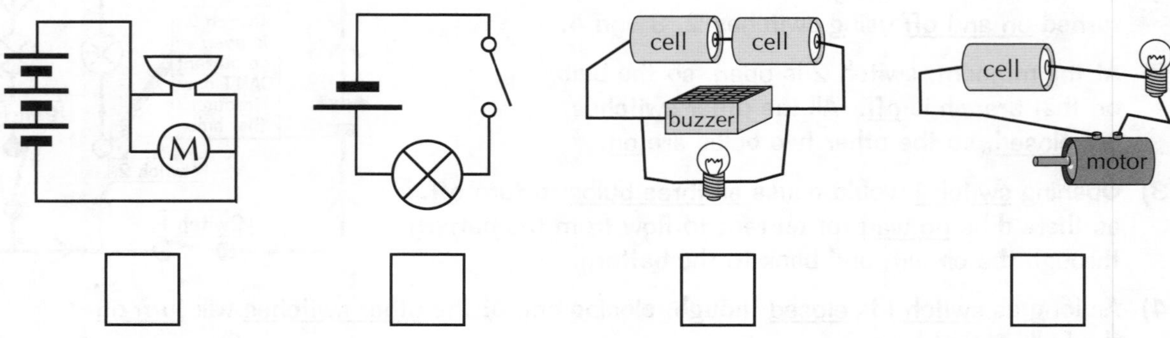

☐ ☐ ☐ ☐

Q3 Look at the circuit below.

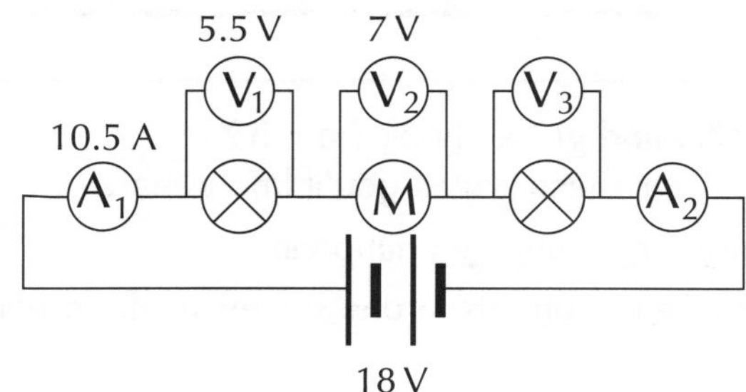

(a) What will the reading on A_2 be? ....

(b) What will the reading on V_3 be? ....

Challenge Yourself

Q4 The parallel circuit shown on the right contains a motor, a bulb, a buzzer and some ammeters.

(a) Complete the table below to show all the ammeter readings.

Ammeter	1	2	3	4	5
Reading (A)	8	2	5		

(b) The same circuit is set up again using different ammeters. One of the new ammeters turns out to have developed a fault. Use the readings below to work out which one it is and explain your answer.

Ammeter	1	2	3	4	5
Reading (A)	13	7	4	10	21

Ammeter .... is faulty because ....

....

....

Q5 The circuit below contains three bulbs and four switches.
Complete the table to show how the bulbs can be controlled by the switches.
The first one has been done for you.

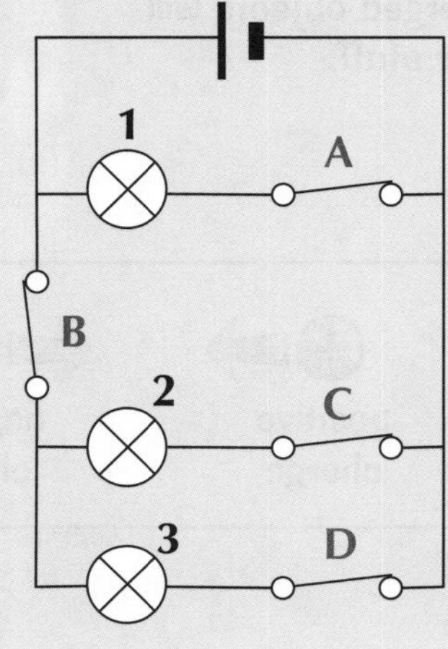

Switches				**Bulbs**		
A	**B**	**C**	**D**	**1**	**2**	**3**
open	closed	closed	closed	off	on	on
closed	open	closed	closed			
closed	closed	open	closed			
closed	closed	closed	open			
closed	closed	open	open			
closed	open	open	closed			
closed	closed	closed	closed			

Topic Review

Did you feel confident answering the questions?
Are you sure you've got all the learning objectives sussed?

Static Electricity

Learning Objectives

Have you ever touched something metallic and got a shock from it? That's a discharge of static electricity. After these pages you'll know that...

- when insulating objects are rubbed together, a separation of charges happens
- this separation of charges is caused by the transfer of electrons from one object to the other
- charged objects have an electric field around them
- charged objects exert forces on other charged objects.

Charges Can Build Up When Objects are Rubbed Together

1) Atoms contain positive and negative charges.
2) The negative charges are electrons. Electrons can move, but positive charges can't.
3) When two insulating objects (see page 84) are rubbed together, the electrons are scraped off one object and left on the other.

The object that gains electrons becomes negatively charged.
The object that loses electrons is left with an equal but positive charge.

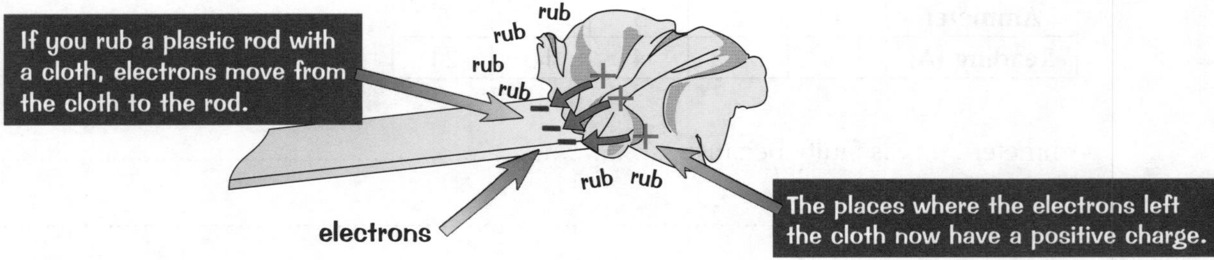

If you rub a plastic rod with a cloth, electrons move from the cloth to the rod.
rub
rub
rub
rub
rub rub
electrons
The places where the electrons left the cloth now have a positive charge.

All Charged Objects Have an Electric Field Around Them

1) Charged objects don't have to touch each other for them to feel a force from each other.
2) An electric field is the space around a charged object where other charged objects will feel a force. That's right, electric forces can act across a gap. Clever stuff.
3) The force charged objects feel when they come near each other depends on what type of charge they have.

Two things with OPPOSITE electric charges are ATTRACTED to each other.
Positive and negative charges attract.

positive charge

negative charge

Two things with the SAME electric charge will REPEL each other.

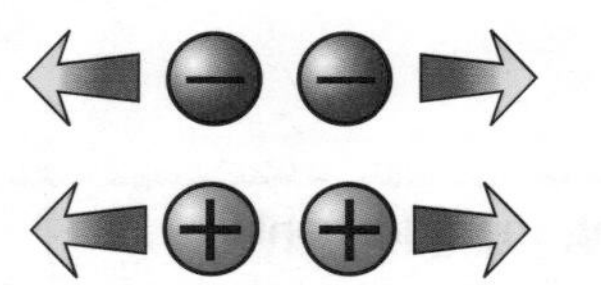

Stupendously Satisfying Static Electricity Questions

Quick Fire Questions

Q1 What kind of charge do electrons have?

Q2 What kind of charges are attracted to positively charged objects?

Practice Questions

Q1 A balloon is rubbed with a piece of cloth.
Afterwards, the balloon attracts objects with a negative charge.

(a) Is the balloon positively or negatively charged after being rubbed with the cloth?

....

(b) What charge does the cloth have after rubbing the balloon?

....

(c) Explain how the balloon and the cloth became charged.

....

....

....

(d) Would the balloon have become charged if it was rubbed with an electrical conductor?

....

Q2 Use words from the box to complete the sentences below.

contact	field	force
positive	negative	

(a) Charged objects have an electric .... around them.

(b) This is a region where other charged objects feel a .... without needing to come in ....

(c) A negatively charged object attracts objects with a .... charge and repels objects with a .... charge.

Topic Review How did you get on with the questions? Have you nailed the learning objectives?   

Magnets

Learning Objectives

I'm sure that you've come across magnets before — but how do they work? Read on to find out. By the end of these pages you'll...

- know that magnets have a north and a south pole
- know that magnets have a magnetic field around them
- be able to draw the magnetic field lines around a magnet
- know how to investigate the magnetic field around a magnet using iron filings or a plotting compass
- know that magnets can be attracted or repelled by each other
- understand that the Earth has a magnetic field and know why a compass helps you navigate.

Magnets are Surrounded by Fields

1) Bar magnets are (surprisingly enough) magnets that are in the shape of a bar. One end of the bar magnet is called the North pole and the other end is called the South pole.
2) All bar magnets have invisible magnetic fields round them.
3) A magnetic field is a region where magnetic materials (e.g. iron) experience a force.
4) You can draw a magnetic field using lines called magnetic field lines. The magnetic field lines always point from the N-pole to the S-pole.
5) This is what the magnetic field around a bar magnet looks like:
6) You can investigate magnetic fields using either iron filings or a plotting compass...

magnetic field lines

N S

North pole

South pole

1) Take some iron filings and scatter them around a bar magnet on a sheet of paper.
2) Iron is magnetic, so the filings will align themselves along the magnetic field lines.

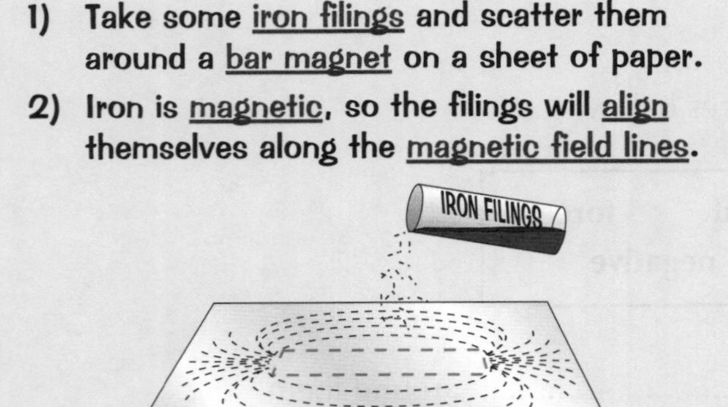

1) Place a magnet flat on a piece of paper.
2) Take a compass and move it around the magnet.
3) The compass will always point from N to S along the field lines wherever it's placed in the field.
4) Remember, The field lines (or "lines of force") always point from NORTH to SOUTH.

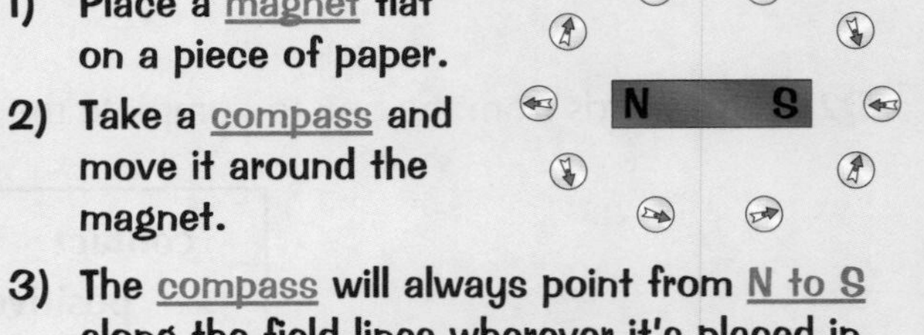

Opposite Poles Attract — Like Poles Repel

Just like electric charges (see page 92), magnets don't need to touch for there to be a force between them.

Attraction

North poles and South poles are attracted to each other.

Repulsion

If you try and bring two of the same type of magnetic pole together, they repel each other.

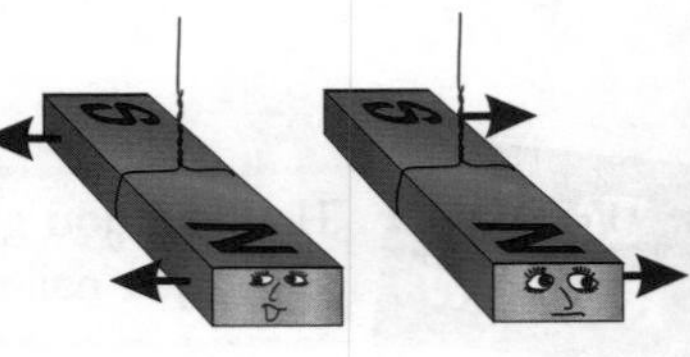

The Earth has a Magnetic Field

1) The Earth has a magnetic field. It has a North pole and a South pole, just like a bar magnet.
2) Compasses line up with magnetic fields — so unless you're stood right next to a magnet, they will point to the Earth's magnetic North pole (which is handily very close to the actual North Pole).
3) Maps always have an arrow on them showing you which direction is North. This means you can use a map and a compass to find your way.

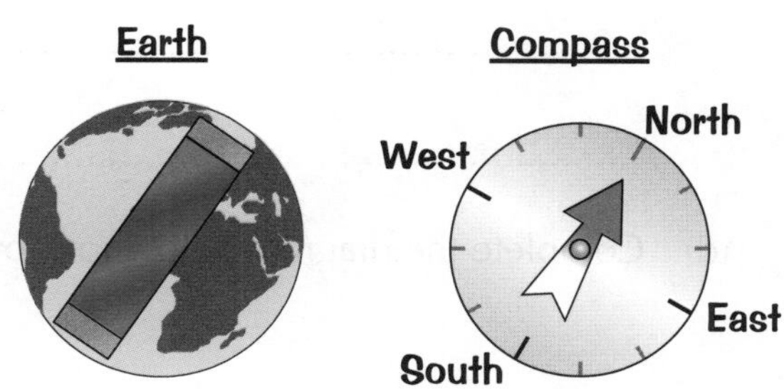

Magically Magnificent Magnet Questions

Quick Fire Questions

Q1 Which way do magnetic field lines point?

Q2 What would happen if you held two magnetic North poles close to each other?

Q3 Why does a compass always point in the same direction when there are no magnets around?

Practice Questions

Q1 (a) Explain what is meant by a magnetic field.

....

....

(b) (i) Describe what will happen to the needle of a compass in a magnetic field.

....

....

(ii) Complete the diagram to show what the compass will look like at these positions around the magnet.

(c) Suggest another way, apart from using a compass, that you can show the magnetic field around a magnet.

....

....

(d) Complete the diagram below to show the field lines around a bar magnet.

S N

Challenge Yourself

Q2 You're given three grey blocks, labelled A, B and C.
They all look the same, but two are magnets and one is a piece of unmagnetised steel.
One end of each block is labelled with an X.
You try placing the blocks next to each of the others in turn, both ways round, and get these results:

A X	X B	→ Repel
A X	B X	→ Attract
X A	B X	→ Repel
X A	X B	→ Attract
A X	X C	→ Attract
A X	C X	→ Attract
B X	X C	→ Attract
B X	C X	→ Attract

Which block is **not** a magnet? Explain your answer.

....

....

....

....

Topic Review

How did you find the questions?
Are you happy with all the learning objectives?

Electromagnets

Learning Objectives

Electromagnets can be a bit tricky to get your head around, so read these pages carefully. After getting through them, you'll know that...

- passing a current through a wire creates a magnetic field around the wire
- magnets made from current-carrying wires are called electromagnets
- a solenoid is a long coil of wire which acts like a magnet when a current goes through it
- you can make DC motors from solenoids.

A Wire With a Current in it Has a Magnetic Field Round it

1) A current going through a wire causes a magnetic field around the wire.

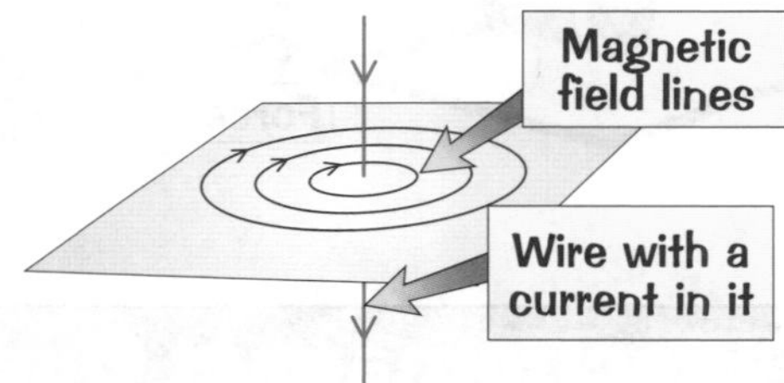

2) Magnets made from a current-carrying wire are called ELECTROMAGNETS.
3) An electromagnet is made from a long coil of wire known as a solenoid.
4) When a current flows through it, the magnetic field of a solenoid is the same as that of a bar magnet:

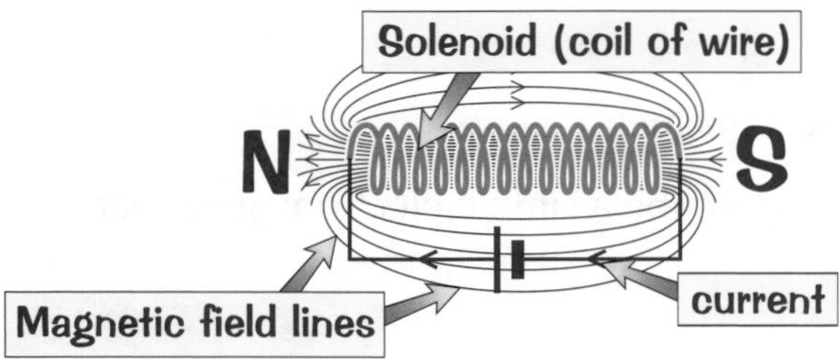

5) Because you can turn the current on and off, the magnetic field can be turned on and off.

You Can Increase the Strength of an Electromagnet

There are three ways to increase the strength of an electromagnet:

1) Put more current through the wire.
2) Put more turns on the solenoid.
3) Put a core of soft iron inside the solenoid.

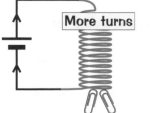

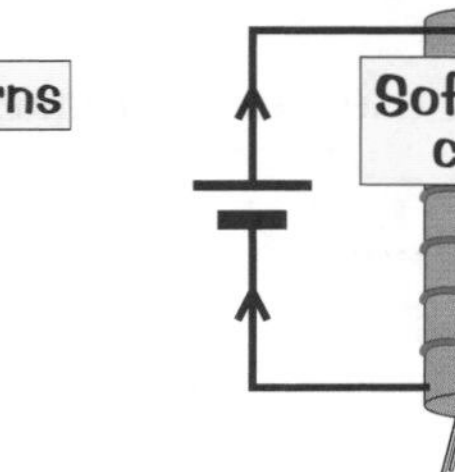

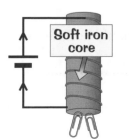

You can't use any metal to make an electromagnet core. You need to use soft iron to make it work as it should (turning on and off when the current is turned on and off).

If you used a steel core, it would stay magnetised after the current was switched off, which would be no good at all.

Electric Motors are Made Using an *Electromagnet*

1) A simple electric motor is made from a loop of coiled wire in a magnetic field.
2) When current flows through the wire, a magnetic field forms around the wire.
3) When this happens, the sides of the coil feel a force from the magnetic field that was already there.
4) The current in each side of the wire flows in opposite directions, so one side is pushed up and the other side is pushed down.
5) This causes the loop of wire to turn — and Bob's your uncle, you've got a motor.

See page 94 for more on the forces magnets exert on each other.

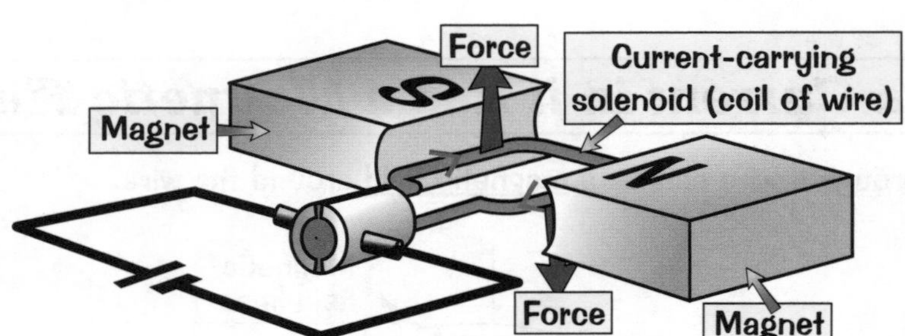

Excitingly Erudite Electromagnet Questions

Quick Fire Questions

Q1 What is an electromagnet?

Q2 Briefly describe how a simple electric motor works.

Practice Questions

Q1 Rajesh is trying to make an electromagnet.

(a) With the help of a diagram, describe a simple electromagnet that Rajesh could make.

....

....

....

(b) Explain why Rajesh should not use steel to make a core for his electromagnet.

....

....

....

Q2 Ted wraps some wire around a cardboard tube to create a solenoid, and connects the solenoid to a battery. The current passing through the solenoid creates a magnetic field.

(a) (i) What is a solenoid?

....

(ii) What has Ted made?

....

(b) Complete the diagram below to show the field lines around the solenoid.

(c) Suggest **three** things Ted could do to increase the strength of the magnetic field.

1. ....

2. ....

3. ....

WS (d) Suggest why Ted should take safety precautions while working with electromagnets.

....

....

WS (e) Suggest **three** precautions Ted could take.

1. ....

2. ....

3. ....

Topic Review

How did you get on with the questions?
Are you confident on all the learning objectives?

Gravity

Learning Objectives

Gravity is the force that keeps your feet firmly on the ground — without it, you'd be scuppered. Once you've read these pages, you'll know...

- that all masses are attracted to each other by the force of gravity
- that the Earth and the Moon, and the Earth and the Sun, are attracted to each other by gravity
- how to calculate the weight of an object from its mass and the gravitational field strength
- that the strength of gravity is different on different planets and stars
- that the gravitational field strength on Earth is about 10 N/kg.

Gravity is a Force that Attracts All Masses

1) Anything with mass will attract anything else with mass. In other words, everything in the Universe is attracted by the force of gravity to everything else. (But you only notice it when one of the things is really big like a planet.)
2) The Earth and Moon are attracted by gravity — that's what keeps the Moon in its orbit.

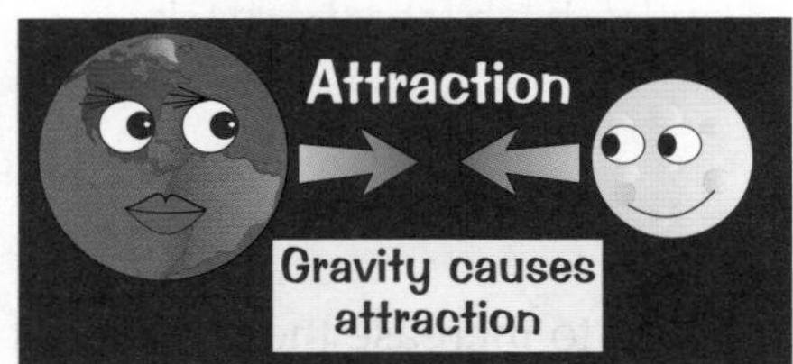

3) The Earth and the Sun are attracted by an even bigger force of gravity.
4) The more massive the object (or body) — the stronger the force of gravity is (so planets with a large mass have high gravity).

Small mass, weak gravity

Medium mass, medium gravity

Large mass, strong gravity

5) The further the distance between objects — the weaker the gravitational attraction becomes.

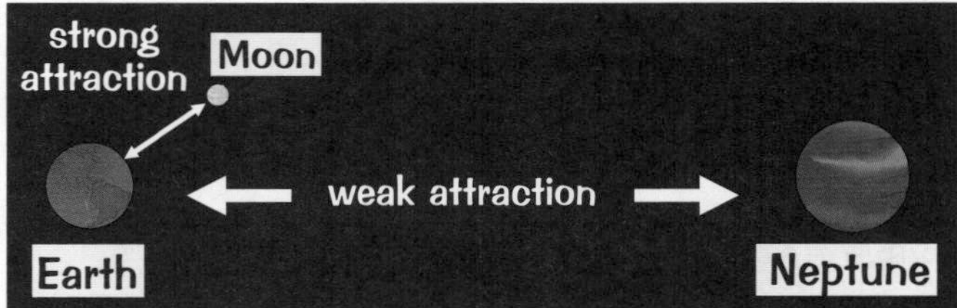

Neptune has a larger mass and stronger gravity than the Moon. But the attraction between Earth and the Moon is much stronger than between Earth and Neptune, because the Moon is much nearer to Earth.

Gravity Gives You Weight — But Not Mass

To understand this you must learn all these facts about mass and weight:

1) Mass is just the amount of 'stuff' in an object.
   The mass of an object never changes, no matter where it is in the Universe.
2) Weight is caused by the pull of gravity.
3) An object has the same mass whether it's on Earth or on another planet (or on a star) — but its weight will be different. For example, a 1 kg mass will weigh less on Mars (about 3.7 N) than it does on Earth (about 10 N), simply because the force of gravity pulling on it is less.

- Weight is a force. It's measured in newtons (N) using a spring balance or newton meter.
- Mass is not a force. It's measured in kilograms (kg) using a mass balance.

N 0 2 4 6 8 10

Learn this Important Formula...

weight = mass × gravitational field strength

in N — in kg — in N/kg

$$W = m \times g$$

1) The letter "g" represents the strength of the gravity and its value is different for different planets. On Earth $g \approx 10$ N/kg. On Mars, where the gravity is weaker, g is only about 3.7 N/kg. On Jupiter, where the gravity is stronger, g is about 25 N/kg.
2) This formula is hideously easy to use:

Example: What is the weight, in newtons, of a 5 kg mass on Earth, on Mars and on Jupiter?

Answer: $W = m \times g$.
On Earth: $W = 5 \times 10 = 50$ N
(The weight of the 5 kg mass is 50 N.)
On Mars: $W = 5 \times 3.7 = 18.5$ N
(The weight of the 5 kg mass is 18.5 N.)
On Jupiter: $W = 5 \times 25 = 125$ N
(The weight of the 5 kg mass is 125 N.)

See what I mean? Hideously easy — as long as you've learnt what all the letters mean.

Gratifyingly Great Gravity Questions

Quick Fire Questions

Q1 What does gravity attract?

Q2 Why does the Moon stay in orbit around the Earth?

Q3 Explain why a 1 kg mass has a different weight on different planets.

Practice Questions

Q1 Complete these sentences by circling the correct words in each set of brackets:

(a) The force of gravity on you is called your (**mass** / **weight**).

(b) If the Earth had a smaller mass, your (**weight** / **mass**) would be less but your (**weight** / **mass**) would stay the same.

(c) Weight is calculated from (**distance** / **mass**) x (**gravitational field** / **mass**) strength.

(d) On Earth the (**gravitational field** / **mass**) strength is about (**ten** / **one**) N/kg.

Q2 Make **one** sentence out of **two** of the phrases below to describe what happens to astronauts when they walk on the Moon.

The astronauts have less weight...

The astronauts have less mass...

...because the Moon's gravity is weaker than Earth's.

...because they are a long way from the Earth.

....

....

Q3 Complete the table showing what these objects would weigh on these bodies in our solar system.

Object	Body	Gravitational Field Strength (N/kg)	Weight (N)
Peter (mass = 60 kg)	Mercury	3.7	
1.5 kg bag of flour	Jupiter	25	
1000 kg car	Uranus	8.7	
100 g apple	Pluto	0.6	

Q4 The Earth is attracted to the Moon and the Sun by gravity.

(a) The strength of the gravitational force between the Earth and the Sun is greater than between the Earth and the Moon, even though the Sun is further away. Explain why.

....

....

....

(b) What is the gravitational field strength on Earth?

....

(c) Would you expect the gravitational field strength on the Sun to be smaller, greater or the same as on the Earth? Explain your answer.

....

....

....

Topic Review **How did you get on with the questions? Have you nailed the learning objectives?** ☐ ☐ ☐

The Sun and Stars

Learning Objectives

Our Sun isn't alone in the Universe — there are loads of other stars out there. Once you've got this page sussed you'll know that...

- the Sun is a star and it's at the centre of our Solar System
- the Sun and lots of other stars make up a galaxy
- there are billions of other galaxies in the Universe
- a light year is how far light travels in one year.

Stars are Giant Balls of Very Hot Gas

1) Stars are extremely massive balls of hot gas held together by gravity.
2) Nuclear reactions inside stars produce lots of energy. That's why they give out light.
3) The Sun is our nearest star. Most stars are so far away that we can't easily see them.
4) The Sun, like all other stars, gives out a huge amount of energy. This heats up the Solar System.

The Sun is at the Centre of Our Solar System

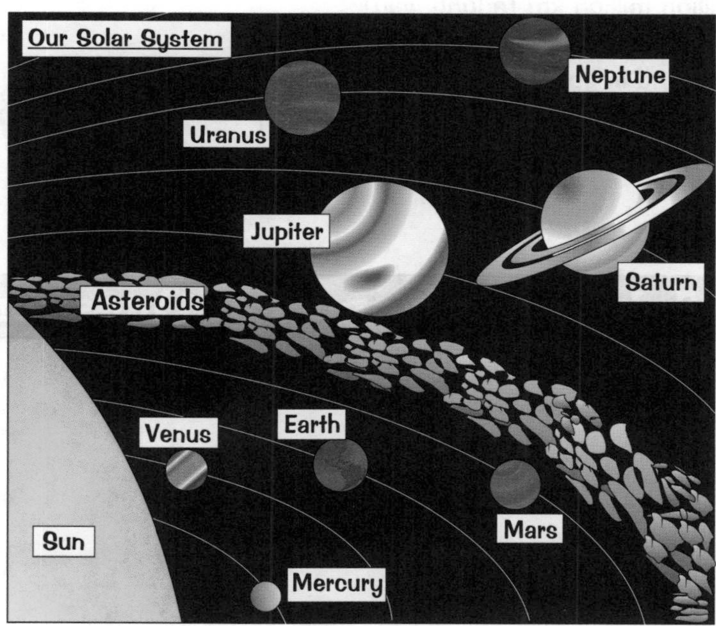

1) A planet is a large body which orbits around a star.
2) The Earth is one of eight planets which orbit the Sun.
3) The Sun is really huge and has a big mass — so its gravity is really strong. The pull from the Sun's gravity is what keeps all the planets in their orbits.
4) The planets all move in elliptical orbits (elongated circles).
5) Planets don't give out light like the Sun and other stars do.

Beyond the Solar System

1) A galaxy is a large collection of stars. The Universe is made up of billions of galaxies.
2) The stars that you see at night are in our own galaxy — the Milky Way. The other galaxies are all so far away they just look like small fuzzy stars.

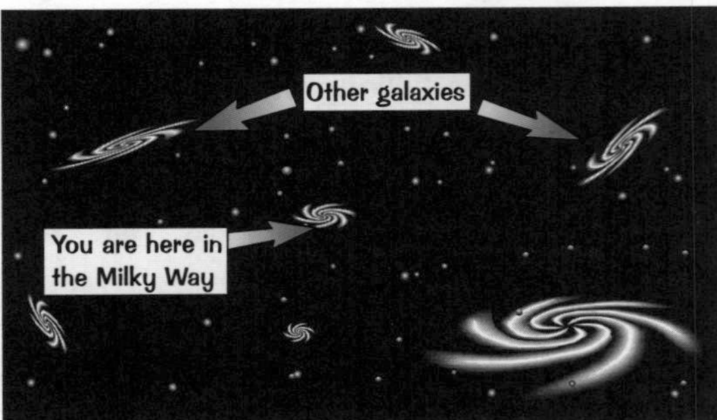

3) There are billions of stars in our galaxy, including the Sun.
4) Other stars in our galaxy include the North Star or Pole Star (which appears in the sky above the North Pole) and Proxima Centauri (our nearest star after the Sun).

A Light Year is a Unit of Distance

1) A light year is how far light travels in one year.
2) 1 light year ≈ 9.5 million million km (a long way)
3) It's used for measuring huge distances between objects — like the distances you find in space.
4) E.g. Proxima Centauri is about 4 light years away, which means it takes light from the star 4 years to reach Earth.

Suspiciously Sublime Sun and Star Questions

Quick Fire Questions

Q1 What is a star?

Q2 What is the nearest star to Earth, other than the Sun?

Q3 What is a light year?

Practice Questions

Q1 Rank these in order of size:

a galaxy	(1) .... (smallest)
the Sun	(2) ....
the Universe	(3) ....
Planet Earth	(4) .... (largest)

Q2 (a) What is a galaxy?

....

(b) What name is given to our own galaxy?

....

(c) Circle the word below that best describes the number of stars in our galaxy:

Tens **Hundreds** **Thousands** **Millions** **Billions** **Trillions**

Q3 Fill in the gaps in these sentences:

(a) The Sun is the star at the centre of our .... System.

(b) The galaxy that the Sun is in is one of .... of galaxies in the Universe.

(c) Other stars in other galaxies are so far away from Earth that the distances are measured in

....

Challenge Yourself

Q4 This table shows the size, mass and amount of light given out by three objects in space, compared to Earth. For each object, write down whether it is a planet, a star or a galaxy. Give a reason for each answer.

Object	Size (diameter)	Mass	Light given out	Explanation
Earth	12 700 km	6×10^{24} kg	None	Doesn't give out light. Fairly small diameter.
....	90 000 light years	?	?	....
....	120 000 km	?	None	....
....	?	2×10^{30} kg	High	....

Topic Review How did you get on with the questions? Are you confident on all the learning objectives?

Day and Night and the Four Seasons

Learning Objectives

By the time you've read and learnt everything there is to know on these pages, you'll be totally great at...

- understanding why the Earth's tilt means we get seasons
- knowing how and why day length changes with the seasons
- appreciating the difference in seasons between the northern and southern hemispheres
- knowing how the rotation of the Earth gives us day and night.

The Seasons are Caused by the Earth's Tilt

1) The Earth takes 365 ¼ days to orbit once around the Sun. That's one year of course. (The extra ¼ day is sorted out every leap year.) Each year has four seasons.
2) The seasons are caused by the tilt of the Earth's axis.

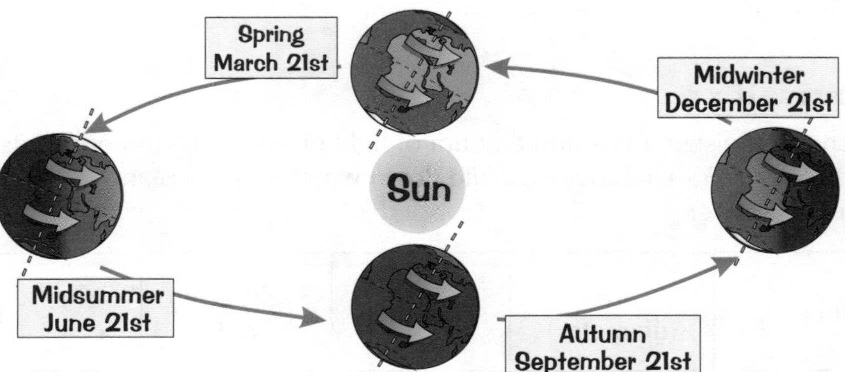

Summer

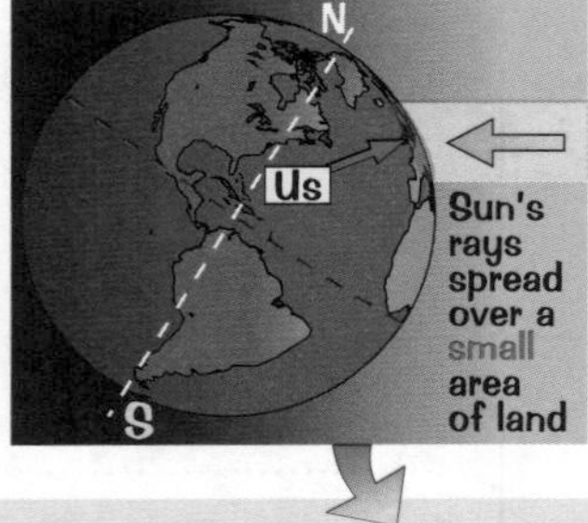

1) When it's summer in the UK, the northern hemisphere (everything above the equator) is tilted towards the Sun.
2) The northern half of the Earth spends more time in sunlight than it does in darkness, i.e. days are longer than nights. Longer days mean more hours of sunshine — so the land heats up.
3) Not only that, but the Sun's rays cover a small area of land. This means that the energy they transfer is focused on a small area. So it gets warm and we have summer — hoorah.

Winter

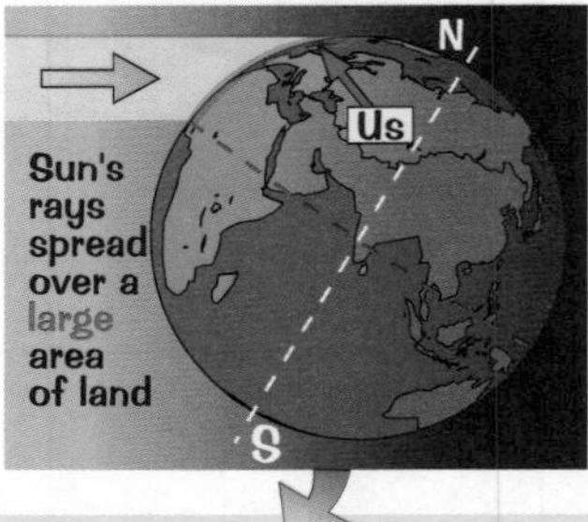

1) When it's winter in the UK, the northern hemisphere is tilted away from the Sun.
2) The north now spends less time in sunlight, so days are shorter than nights.
3) Also, the Sun's rays cover a larger area of land, so the energy they transfer is more spread out. So it gets colder and we have winter.

When it's summer in the northern hemisphere, it's winter in the southern hemisphere — and vice versa.

Day and Night are Due to the Steady Rotation of The Earth

1) The Earth does one complete rotation in 24 hours. That's what a day actually is — one complete rotation of the Earth about its axis.
2) The Sun doesn't really move, so as the Earth rotates, any place on its surface (like England, say) will sometimes face the Sun (day time) and other times face away into dark space (night time).

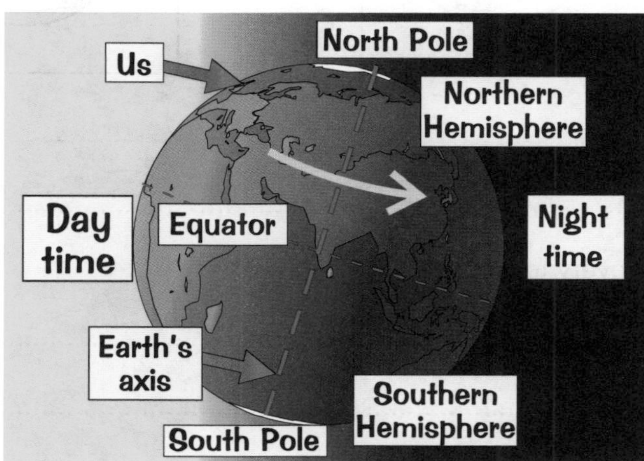

Dapper Day, Nifty Night and Super Season Questions

Quick Fire Questions

Q1 What causes seasons?

Q2 How long does it take the Earth to orbit the Sun completely?

Q3 Why are days shorter in winter?

Q4 How long is one complete rotation of the Earth?

Practice Questions

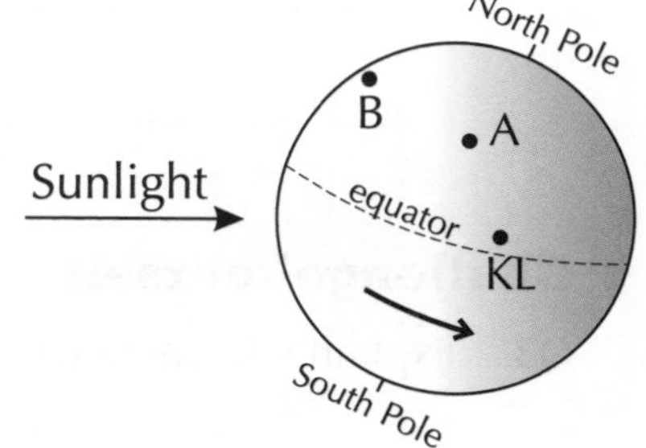

Q1 The picture on the right shows the Earth at a particular moment in time. In the picture, Birmingham is labelled **B**, Astana is labelled **A** and Kuala Lumpur is labelled **KL**.

(a) Use the diagram to explain how, at the time shown in the picture, night time is changing to day time in Astana.

....

....

....

(b) Look at the four statements below. Write **B** next to the one that **best describes** the time of day in Birmingham at this moment. Write **KL** next to the one that **best describes** the time of day in Kuala Lumpur at this moment. (Do not write anything next to the other two statements.)

It is midday. .... The Sun has just set. ....

It is midnight. .... The Sun will rise soon. ....

Q2 The diagrams below show the Earth at different times in a year.

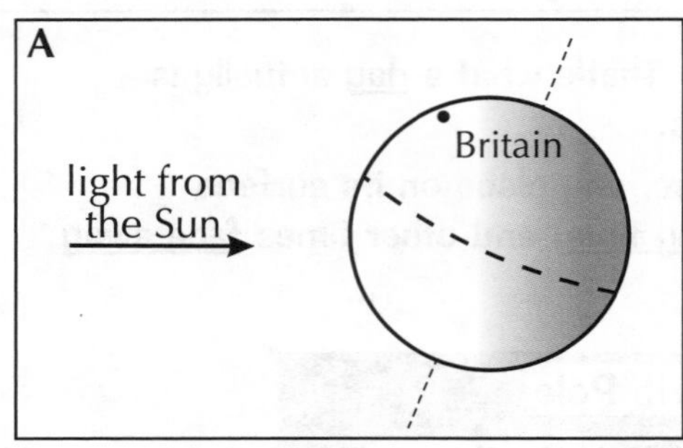

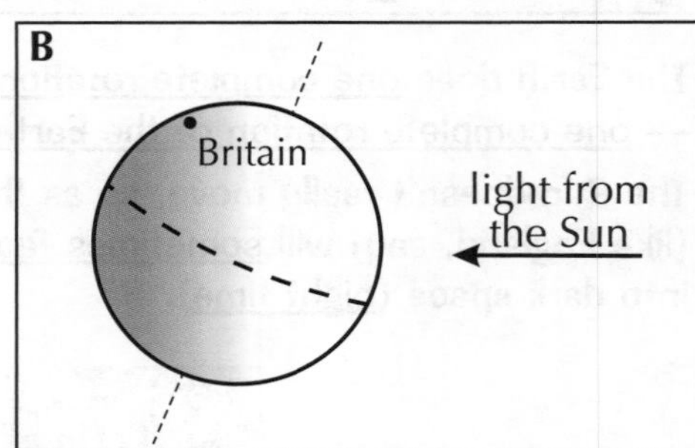

(a) (i) What is a year?

....

(ii) Explain why every fourth year is a leap year.

....

....

(b) Which diagram, A or B, shows Britain when it is

(i) summer? .... (ii) winter? ....

(c) When the northern hemisphere is tilted **away** from the Sun, in what **two** ways is the daylight different to when it is tilted towards the Sun?

1 ....

2 ....

(d) Explain why it is summer in the southern hemisphere when it is winter in the northern hemisphere.

....

....

Challenge Yourself

Q3 Explain why there would be no seasons if the Earth was not tilted.

....

....

....

....

....

Topic Review

Did you sail through the questions without any trouble?
Are you sure you understand all of the learning objectives?

Index

Index